SCRATCHING
YOUR ENTREPRENEURIAL
ITCH

SCRATCHING
YOUR ENTREPRENEURIAL
ITCH

*A Guide
to Business
Venturing*

Peter C. Channing

HAWTHORN BOOKS, INC.
Publishers / NEW YORK

SCRATCHING YOUR ENTREPRENEURIAL ITCH

Library of Congress Catalog Card Number 77-84974

ISBN: 0-8015-6607-X

1 2 3 4 5 6 7 8 9 10

"If one advances confidently
in the direction of his dreams,
and endeavors to live the life
which he has imagined,
he will meet with success
unexpected in common hours."

Thoreau

CONTENTS

FOREWORD

It seems ironic in a country whose socio-economic superiority has evolved through the entrepreneurial efforts of the individual that so little is known about the person we call ... entrepreneur.

Entrepreneurship is not really viewed as a creative endeavor by academia. The "self-employed" individual is considered the poorest of credit risks; the undertaking of a new enterprise commands little or no institutional financial assistance. On a comparative income scale with his corporate (and professional) counterpart, the entrepreneur is poorly statused. It is only *after* his endeavors have produced material possessions in abundance that he is ever accorded any relative semblance of "equality or desirability" in our society.

The significance of the complaint is fear. Are we discouraging individual venturing via the premium placed on corporate careers? Is the function of business being reduced to one of management? Will we now evolve a society whose business acumen is lodged almost singularly in the corporation with venturing reserved for the tradesman, the uneducated and the corporation? If so, do we impair or endanger the underpinnings of our system of free enterprise? I propose these questions apolitically and without answers. But, I believe them to be questions worthy of serious examination by all sectors of the business community.

I have two express hopes for this book. First, and foremost, that people who are considering their initial venture will have the odds for success firmly shifted in their favor. Secondly, that there might be some stimulation in the academic community to do a better job of relating personality, per se, and the psychological aspects of business to the fundamentals of business so as to more adequately prepare the individual who would undertake entrepreneurial ventures.

I am indeed grateful to all my business associates, friends and other entrepreneurs for their encouragement, support and assistive critique. A very special note of thanks is due my secretary "B.G."

To my family whose memory banks bear full traumatic testimony to my credentials for this book, I can best say ... BLESS!

Peter C. Channing

SCRATCHING
YOUR ENTREPRENEURIAL
ITCH

I
INSIGHT

Thousands upon thousands of business failures each year. I sure as hell wasn't alone. No ... I was *very much* alone. Indeed, I had never felt so alone in my life. Or so terribly frightened. Scarcely a year ago, I was on the way to what promised to be an incredibly successful business venture. On this day, I have absolutely nothing left. No money, no job and zero prospects for either. The financial aspect of the failure seems to pale in comparison to the other loss ... I have no direction for the future and my self-confidence is non-existent.

I watch the wind-flattened waters of the bay curl open for the bow of the small borrowed sailboat and wonder about them as an alternative. But just momentarily. Three things immediately dissuade me. What can "they" do to me ... kill me? They can't take something away from me I don't have. And, I'm just plain curious to see what I'm going to do about my predicament. (If nothing else, the water is just too damn cold.) Suddenly, I'm reminded of a favorite expression of a close friend which he often uses to convey the potential effect of something unpleasant ... "it'll make you wish you'd died as a baby." And I think I do ... almost ... wish I had.

It has been almost a full week now since the final shut down of the business. On the one hand, I know perfectly well what happened; I've overlaid the situation with all the reasons we're told businesses fail, e.g., lack of capital, poor management, etc., etc., and see similarities, but that isn't enough. Something (important for me to understand) is missing. And though I sense impending discovery, whatever I need to understand lies tantalizingly just beneath the surface; demanding yet defying recognition. Like an unremembered name whose recall is hastened by cessation of effort, I let go of whatever it is I'm trying to identify and turn my attention back to the sea.

The sun seems to quicken its set and I begin a slow reach back on an ever slightening breeze. I recall another day, many years ago now, that held weather like this. I was teaching my oldest son to sail.
"What makes the boat go, Daddy?"

"The wind pushes on the sail ... up there," I said.

He watched the sail for a while and then, with a look of puzzlement on his face asked, "But why does it go, Daddy?"

I was just driving through the gates of the sailing club when it struck me ... my son's question about why a boat sails. That was it! That was what I didn't understand about my business failure. WHY! *Why* did I do ... or not do? If I had run out of money (which I had), *why* had I? Any fool knows that under-capitalization is a leading cause of business failures. So, it really isn't enough to just know what business statistic(s) occurred.

Business failure statistics. I began to realize they didn't tell me a damn thing ... not really. Even worse, they were of absolutely no use to me. The more I thought about it, the more convinced I became that these so-called *reasons* were nothing more than statistical end-products; compiled and presented by people who had no earthly idea as to WHY their data occurred. They only knew the result. Like reading that an airliner, on final approach, in heavy weather, undershoots the runway and crashes. That's *what* happened. WHY it happened is the critical thing to be understood!

Weeks later, after having analyzed *why* I had failed, I could say this failure (as well as my others) was, to a very great degree, completely unnecessary! The intervening years, and subsequent successes, have proven I was right. I also know thousands of other business failures are unnecessary. In fact, there is no such thing as a *business* failure ... BUSINESSES DON'T FAIL ... *people* fail!

ABOUT THIS BOOK

core statemt

Thesis: The thesis of this book is that if qualified people venture forth, for the proper reasons, armed with knowledge of the many subtle and insidious pitfalls that either induce or contribute to failure, there would be far fewer failures.

Purpose: The purpose of this book then, succinctly stated, is to share with the reader INSIGHTS into the evolvement and conduct of entrepreneurial ventures that could provide that critical margin of difference between success and failure.

The result should be to encourage, and help prepare, those who have sound, basic entrepreneurial attributes and motivations. Those who shouldn't venture forth will hopefully be discouraged from doing so. If the book is successful, your chances for success will be greatly increased (regardless of whether your decision is to become an entrepreneur or remain in corporate life)!

Uniqueness: There are two interrelated reasons why this book is unique. First, we're dealing with some propositions not customarily or classically associated with business (probably because the simplistic nature thereof masks importance which, in turn, precludes easy recognition). The second reason, which makes a lot of sense when you think about it, is this: The *successful* entrepreneur, if he's telling you anything, is busy recounting his success. *Text books* are most often written by people "unblooded" in the world of the entrepreneur. The *unsuccessful* entrepreneur, the most likely source of understanding failure, may well not *know* why he failed. Or, if he does, he's not interested in telling the world (why) he failed.

What it is not: This book is clearly not presented nor intended as an all-inclusive technical treatise. There is hardly any aspect of the technicalities of the business world that is not covered by innumerable scholarly works by very knowledgeable, very capable people. They are readily available for study and reference and I urge the use thereof. But, apparently ... obviously ... that isn't enough. For, if mere possession of knowledge in these technical areas were sufficient, most everyone, at least theoretically, could/would be successful in business.

3

For Whom it was Written: It is generally intended for the person who is presently working for the *corporation* (or who has recently left the corporation in a venture of his or her own). The significance of this particular audience is most clearly and effectively explained by categorizing the four broad types of entrepreneurs we have in this country.

(1) The (Large) Corporation: These are concerns that possess relatively unlimited resources in every aspect of a new undertaking.

(2) The "Wealthy" Individual: This is the person who, whether through inherited, earned or married wealth, has sufficient assets at his disposal. Absent is the risk of losing everything. He never has to bet the roof over his children's heads or the food in their stomachs; or very much of his ego or career.

(3) Those Who Have No Choice: These are people who are "forced" into becoming entrepreneurs. They are probably "unemployable" (for whatever reasons) at the level of income they desire/require and *have no alternative* but to go into a business of their own.

(4) Middle Income-Middle Management-Middle America: The corporate "animal." Some savings or investments perhaps, but limited. The *option* of a successful corporate career is theirs! Yet, this person thinks and dreams about being on his own ... being free from the corporation ... doing his thing. The itch is there. When and if he does venture forth on his own, *he'll lay everything right up on the line*. It is to this person then, who has little else but an idea and desire, nothing to fall back on, everything to lose and the option to "stay where it's safe" that this book is directed.

It is also intended for those who will become involved with your plans (and the ultimate venture should you decide to go forth). Your wife, attorney, CPA, investors, lenders, etc., should be as aware of this material as you are. Why? Because if they understand and appreciate what's contained in this book, one of two things will occur. They'll be far more helpful and understanding in and of a venture. Or,

4

if you're (obviously) not the entrepreneurial type, they may be entitled, for everyone's sake, to try and dissuade you.

I submit to the professional reader that *his* assessment of a client's chances (of success) when considered in terms of the material in this book would indeed be beneficial. I think there are many failures where advisors, whatever their capacity, must share (if they're perfectly honest), a portion of the "blame." I'm speaking of those instances where the client is well known to the professional. And the professional has a pretty good idea the client may not be suited to the undertaking. (There were absolutely times when I, as a financial advisor, should have tried to suggest to a client he might want to "think about a situation twice." So I'm familiar with the reasons why you "shouldn't.") Certainly, it's a delicate situation. So is taking the car keys away from a drunk friend.

Why Do People Fail as Entrepreneurs?

The people-failure factors reduce down to an *absence of*:

(1) SOUND MOTIVATION FOR BECOMING AN ENTREPRENEUR.

(2) ENTREPRENEURIAL TALENT.

(3) AWARENESS OF VARIOUS PSYCHOLOGICAL PITFALLS.

The next three chapters deal respectively and specifically with these problem areas. The remaining chapters consider the entrepreneurial aspects of traditional business subjects from·a practical or common sense point of view.

This I promise you. If you get through this book with honesty and objectivity and still feel you're capable of mounting a successful venture, your chances of doing so will be greatly enhanced. If, on the other hand, you lay aside this book at any given point with a feeling of despondence (or having rejected a majority of the premise), you may be making the most serious of mistakes to proceed with your venture.

II

MOTIVATION

This is where it begins. Success or failure. You've got to be right at the outset. If your motivation for becoming an entrepreneur is not valid, you will, most probably, fail. Going into business, or doing your own thing, on your own is a deadly serious proposition. Your motivation will form the foundation, and thus the strength, of your venture. It is impossible to ascertain just how many otherwise categorized reasons for failure, e.g., insufficient funding, lack of management, etc., are, in reality, statistical excuses for faulty motivation. But, you may be certain, the number is substantial.

Since, as I've indicated, there are no hard statistical (business) data to support this thesis, how valid is the contention? For the answer, we have to turn to the psychological community and common sense. When you think about it, it isn't too difficult to agree that the fundamental impetus in the consideration of an entrepreneurial venture is *fantasy*. Now, if we accept the dictionary's definition of fantasy, "a supposition based on no solid foundation" or "imagination," etc., we're getting somewhere. You're right, the would-be entrepreneur *must* fantasize. How else could the process begin. From what other "source" does one project himself, ultimately, into the possibility of something. However, it's at this precise stage or mental state that the individual is most vulnerable to reality-error. He's in a state of fantasy. The danger is that his *entire world* can become fantasy oriented. (Like a game of toy soldiers. When all your troops are killed, you just stand them back up and go again.)

Since nothing is "real" yet, potential problem areas are often either completely over-looked or unrealistically discounted. Whatever it takes to get-on-with-it is in the order of the day. Omnipotence reigns supreme. It's a wonderful time, a delicate time, and a potentially lethal time.

The solution may be more easily stated than executed. Get your head out of the clouds; try and find the compromise position of *realistic* fantasy, to coin a phrase. You don't want to lose the fantasy, and thus the impetus, but you *must* induce reality in terms of yourself and the project. Think of it this way. Fantasy inevitably disappears anyway, sooner or later. One of three things will happen:

(a) You forget about the proposition entirely.

(b) You reduce fantasy to a realistic dream and pursue its success.

(c) You pursue an unrealistic fantasy to realistic failure.

Only one of these alternatives holds any promise of a successful venture. *Now* is the time to investigate, test, analyze and reconsider your primary or fundamental reason(s) for deciding to become an entrepreneur.

NEGATIVE MOTIVATIONS:

(1) You Don't Like Corporate Life:

If this is your chief reason for pursuing a business venture of your own, you could be headed for deep trouble. To be sure, being an entrepreneur is an alternative to "institutional" life. The question may be, which of the two represents the greater problem for you? If you're running away *from* the corporation vis-a-vis *to* your own operation, I can almost promise you that you've chosen the greater evil. Chances are extremely good that you're going to find out first hand, exactly how the "matador" feels with 1,000 pounds of livestock bearing down on him at thirty miles an hour when all he wanted to do was wear tight pants and hear a crowd cheer.

(2) You're Not Doing too Well in Your Present Job:

Same idea as number one. You're going to find yourself in that unexpected bull ring.

(3) Money Only:

Don't be dumb. Nobody, if they're "normal," does anything (legitimate) *solely* for money. As a management consultant once said to me, "If you're *only* in business to make money, you're in the wrong business; you ought to be in crime. Sky-high profit margins, no taxes ... women, dope, gambling ... big, big, money!"

The point is, facetiously, well made. It's amazing though how many people are motivated by what they perceive as being an unlimited avenue to wealth. What kind of money do you expect to make with your venture?

If you figure 10% to 15% net before taxes on an operation is excellent, which it usually is, how would you feel about 5%, or breakeven ... or a loss? Of course, your salary comes out before that, but how much can you afford to draw down? $25,000? $35,000? $50,000? There's a limit. All I'd like for you to do is consider your present corporate salary as a percentage of, say, a half-million dollars. Then relate the answer to a realistic "take" from your own proposed business. Secondly, don't lose sight of the fact that as you project your earnings from a private venture out five or ten years, you must also project where you'd be in the corporation. This simple exercise will be helpful in gaining the proper perspective for the money end of an entrepreneurial consideration. When your corporate salary is considered in the light of how much you'd have to have invested to give you the same return, you may decide your job is a pretty good investment. (Especially on a risk-reward basis!)

In any event, one of the worst mistakes the average person can make is to decide to "do his own thing" simply for money.

(4) Freedom:

From what? You can dress pretty much as you like (unless it bothers your customers). You can take time off whenever you like (unless you have to be there as the key person to see that things function). You don't have to put up with company politics (unless your prospects, customers, suppliers, bankers, etc. have politics in their operations). You're free to make your own bright decisions (if you don't need the financial integrity of a large corporation to "underwrite" your mistakes). Well, I'm sure you understand what I'm saying. We really never get completely free from the things that "bug" us about corporate life. Or, if we do, we acquire other restrictions that off-set. And yet, I, of course, know what we all mean when we talk about the "freedom" that comes from being on your own. It's just that this freedom, *in and of itself,* is no criterion for becoming an entrepreneur. Remember, you've got some pretty nice freedoms in the corporation, e.g., freedom from worry about where the next paycheck is coming from, freedom to get sick, to take vacations, to make (some) expensive mistakes, etc. etc.

(5) Just Want To Try:

Well, this can be a pretty compelling reason. Especially when you reach the middle years (whatever they are) and begin to sense, or actually become quite concerned with, time slipping by and you've never even "tried." You've just talked and hoped and dreamed. Then, too, there's the younger age group who "want to try it" while they're young — before they get "too old and tired." But just wanting to try is not a good enough reason, per se, to go tearing off out there. Let it be just what it should be ... this just wanting-to-try urge ... simply the impetus to start you seriously considering all the aspects of taking such a risk. *If* you find that you have the attributes of an entrepreneur and your concept is viable ... *then* I think just wanting to do it may be a good reason to get on with it!

(6) Compelled To Try:

All I can say here is be extremely cautious. *Why* are you compelled to try. If you can think it through and honestly know why and the reason is sound ... Okay. But, I'd certainly urge you to consider seeking an objective, learned opinion.

(7) Your Only Option:

This usually is a result (though not always) of job depression. Not feeling good about yourself in what you're doing. The career is sagging. You've made some dumb mistakes, been passed over for promotion, tried to find another job with little or no success. And, unlike the big boys in the locker room, you're not being sought after by companies offering elaborate deals. In fact, nobody wants you ... period. Well, that can, and does, happen to almost all of us at one time or another. And it's very real. But the answer does *not* lie in becoming an entrepreneur. You may make an excellent entrepreneur; that's not the point. The point is ... don't let a situation like this cause you to decide to try something unless you first take full measure of your abilities as an entrepreneur. Then you'll be moving *to* something on the proper basis! To be sure, history is filled with people who "couldn't" or didn't make it in the corporation and, as a result, turned to entrepreneurship and were resounding successes. The key though is, they were *entrepreneurially talented!* Are you? Better to "fail" or be "unsuccessful" in the corporation, where you can still eat and pay the rent, then to ... well, you understand.

(8) Adventure, Romance, Etc.:

It's an adventure alright. So is being hip deep in alligators in a Florida swamp. Romantic? I do seem to recall, in my single days, a lovely romantic evening with a young lady with whom I had been enamored for many months. It was romantic; just as I had thought it would be. I also will carry to the grave that feeling I experienced upon saying hello to the husband I didn't know she had, in his own living room!

I've only treated this area lightly because I'm very certain you're not really going to make a decision to become an entrepreneur because of adventure and romance.

(9) My Father Told Me That Was The Way:

I'm not about to go around knocking fathers. If I had listened (if we all had or would), I'd probably be a lot better off. But, again, you have to measure *yourself* against whether *you* have what it takes. Chasing family "ghosts," living or dead, is decidely detrimental to one's financial health.

(10) If He Did ... I Can:

This could well be the biggest Judas goat of all. Because anytime you talk about the other fellow's achievements, what you're really talking about *is* the man. HE is the achievement. Thus, to say, "if he did, I can," is to suggest that you are that man. The inference is, you're superior, or at least equal, to him. Well, you may be ... in all that's visible. But, just don't forget there are an infinite number of things you can't or don't see about this person. If nothing else, he may have been too dumb to know he couldn't! And that's *his* edge. (I'll have more to say about this topic in a later chapter.)

(11) I Can Always Go Back To What I Left:

Don't be too sure! It may be a great deal more difficult than you could ever conceive. But, that's what a lot of us say, and have said to us. To the extent that it may be true for you, it is *only* something extra that's nice to have. It is not a valid, primary reason for becoming an entrepreneur; nor should it be the deciding factor that weights a decision to venture forth.

———— o ————

These are some of the reasons why you should *not* become an entrepreneur. While it may be true one or more of these reasons have been responsible for starting some on the road to success, they've also sent many thousands more into financial and emotional oblivion. If I've stifled a dream you've had at this point, that's all you really had anyway ... a dream.

POSITIVE MOTIVATIONS:

There are any number of good reasons, sound reasons, for you to be considering the entrepreneurial route. Among them are:

(1) The invention or development or improvement of a (new) product or service that can be proven viable.

(2) Recognition of how you might be able to compete with an existing product or service through cost reductions unavailable to or impossible for the competition.

(3) "Popular Demand," which is to say that some people are so obviously good at something, they are continually encouraged by others to break away on their own. (This can be misleading however, and we'll talk more about it in a later chapter.)

(4) You may just really want to. I did say earlier that this was not justifiable or a good reason. And I don't think it is, in and of itself. But, I don't want to stifle that urge or desire that may not initially manifest itself with an idea of exactly what it is you're going to do. On the contrary, I would urge you to carefully and systematically pursue the urge or feeling in terms of figuring out what you might do ... what you could do. *Most* importantly, are you the entrepreneurial type?

(5) Being "forced" into taking the entrepreneurial route is not an unacceptable reason under the right circumstances. I'm speaking specifically about the forty-plus year old who finds himself out of the (acceptable) job market. This can be legitimate motivation *provided* he is qualified to undertake an entrepreneurial venture!

Just because I may not have included your specific reason or motivation does not, of course, render it invalid. The purpose of this chapter is not to destroy dreams but to encourage examination thereof. You must believe it is critically important to fully understand your motivation for wanting to be in business for yourself.

Being an entrepreneur is about as for real a situation as life offers. Never doubt for a moment that you aren't going to be putting most of those things we all hold very dear at great risk. You will be going in "Harm's Way" ... make sure WHY makes sense!

III

THE ENTREPRENEUR

People fail ... businesses don't. There is no better or more appropriate way to begin this chapter. Because it's most unlikely that entrepreneurial success ever comes to those who are not entrepreneurially talented; anymore than success in any field comes to the unqualified who attempt participation therein. If we had as many unqualified people permitted to fly aircraft, perform surgery, teach in our schools, operate machines, play in our orchestras, etc., as we do undertake entrepreneurial ventures, this country would probably cease to function after a time.

But, in our society, no credentials are required for entrepreneurship; it's open to any and everyone ... and it should be. The problem, of course, is, the same ease with which one can enter the world of business-on-his-own, so can he exit.

If we want to reduce to a single common denominator the reason for most people failing in business, we can simply say, "They didn't know what in the hell they were doing." The big idea comes along, "in" they go, and before they even have time to realize what's happening, they're beat about the head and shoulders unmercifully by "things" they never dreamed existed. When you're in business for yourself, you're in a rough and tumble world where only the very fit are going to stand any chance of survival.

In my view then, you ought to stop right here and, for the moment, forget about how great your deal is and why you want to pursue it. The vital question is ... can *YOU* bring it off. Self-deception runs rampant in the early stages of a proposition, but there's salvation in the mere recognition of that fact ... if you'll embrace the objectivity required to manifest it. And that's what this chapter offers you. The opportunity and the means to measure yourself against the fundamental characteristics time and experience have proven an individual must have if he is going to be an entrepreneurial success.

PERSONAL CHARACTERISTICS:

The *attitude* with which you approach this section will serve as an excellent indicator of whether or not you have "what it takes" to be an entrepreneur. If you're inclined to simply brush it off with an "aw, hell, I've got what it takes," you're probably involved in a serious act of self-deception. Don't just read through these criteria. Take your time! Think about each one ... about your *first* impression of yourself as you read a given benchmark. Additionally, it will be most advantageous if you can recall specific experiences in the past that directly relate to each characteristic. Wherever that's vague or impossible, you can at least imagine a circumstance and project yourself into it. (For example, if you've always been accustomed to arriving home about 6:00 p.m., for a ritual dinner with the family, and time after with the children, how is 8:00 p.m. or 9:00 p.m. with no time for the children going to set ... with them and you?)

Rate yourself on a scale of one to ten for each characteristic. After you've finished, forget this part of the book for a few days. Then, come back and rate yourself again; without looking at the first rating. Next, compare the two ratings. Where there are wide differences in any specific category, it probably won't be too difficult to determine why ... but you should make a concerted effort to understand the variance. If you conclude this portion of the evaluation with an overall rating of a 7 or 8, you're ready to move to the last phase of the analysis.

Finally (and perhaps most importantly), you should discuss *your* rating with several people who you feel know you pretty well, e.g.,

16

your wife, business friends, your attorney, your banker, etc. Tell them *why* you rated yourself as you did. What do they think? Would they rate you any differently and, if so, how? (I would, however, caution you to keep in mind the observations about friends noted in the next chapter.) If you "emerge" from this final phase of the exercise with a composite rating on the high side, say a 7 or 8, then I think you possess sufficient entrepreneurial talent to proceed with the determination of whether you have a viable venture.

(1) Self-Confidence:

You should be a person who feels good about himself, is (realistically) supremely confident, and believes he, rather than others or things, controls what happens to him in his life time.   *10*

(2) Perseverance:

Have there been instances in your life where you've had to demonstrate the ability to "keep getting up off the floor" and staying after something despite continual discouragement and disappointment? How did you feel about it?

Perseverance is critical to entrepreneurial success! You must have this capacity if you're going into business for yourself.

(3) Flexibility:

I like to define this as the capability for alternative thought and action which induces constructive reality into perseverance.

(4) Common Sense:

We all know what this is. The problem lies in the fact that those who don't have it aren't usually aware they don't. How many times have we all heard it said of someone, "Oh, he's as bright as they come ... he just doesn't have any *common* sense." Well, I'll bet *he* thinks he does. In any event, you had best have a generous helping of it. This is one area of personal evaluation you should pay particular attention to in terms of how others rate you!

17

(5) High Energy Level:

The entrepreneur especially must be capable of sustained periods of long, arduous (and productive) hours. Take a moment and look around at any person who is really successful (at whatever he does). He's always a person blessed with a high energy level.

(6) Problem Solving:

You should both enjoy and excel at finding solutions to problems. The success of moving a project through to completion depends upon your ability to solve problems. If you're easily discouraged by problems ... if they throw you into a funk ... if you don't or can't view them as a natural part of any process ... then, you'll be in for some terribly trying times as an entrepreneur.

(7) Commitment:

You should have the capacity to commit to relatively long term propositions ... of at least five years duration. It has been said that of all men in the world, entrepreneurs are the most committed. Without the ability to make and discharge commitments, you'll be extremely vulnerable to the fickle winds of day to day operations which can occasionally be strong and unpleasant enough to cause project abandonment.

(8) "Delegation"

You have to be both willing and able to effectively utilize the minds and talents of other people inside, as well as outside, your organization. You should believe in and be able to actualize a philosophy of, "If I can surround myself with people brighter than I am, they will make me successful." If you have a strong tendency to "do it all yourself," you will, at least, bear unnecessary problems, and, at best, not be as successful as you could be.

(9) Tolerance For Risk:

Obviously, you should have a high tolerance for risk. An entrepreneur's security must lie within himself vis-a-vis a bank account. But, an entrepreneur is not a gambler, per se. He is interested in *moderate* risks because he's an *achiever* and can only fulfill that need through achieving. Winning a *gamble* is not viewed as something achieved, per se.

(10) High Learning Curve:

The ability to learn new things quickly to a functional level will prove to be most important. Being in business for yourself requires the expansion of one's capabilities into areas the average corporate executive has not been exposed in terms of total responsibility.

(11) Initiative:

If you can't move yourself, or don't enjoy taking matters in hand, you absolutely do not belong in the entrepreneurial arena. There *is* no one else but you. If you attempt to depend on others to take the lead or prompt *you,* your venture will not last very long.

(12) Failure:

An entrepreneur must be able to look at failure as a learning experience and possess an attendant ability to apply lessons learned from failure to the future. You must neither fear failure nor be discouraged by it.

(13) Money:

Is not the end that justifies the means to the entrepreneur. Rather, *what* you do should be the reason you do it, with financial rewards being only a yardstick of how well you did it.

(14) Responsibility:

You must want it, thrive on it, always be willing and anxious to embrace it. Responsibility in the corporate strata, regardless of its magnitude, is (somehow) never quite equal in terms of the personal impact it can make if one has an aversion to it.

(15) Decision Making:

You have to like it and be good at it. The ability to make sound judgments, on limited data, in a timely manner, under (sometimes extreme) pressure is obviously critical to a successful venture. If you dislike making decisions, or must have everything quantified prior thereto (or have a strong historical tendency toward vacillation), you may be well advised to reconsider your decision to venture forth on your own.

(16) Realistic Goals and Standards:

You must be capable of extracting realistic and definable goals from your dream, as well as setting standards for yourself against which you compete in the pursuit of these established goals. This does not conflict with the school of thought that urges the setting of goals "outside one's reach," unless that old saying defines the phrase to mean *un*reachable. I believe in *stretching* but only to the extent that I realistically have a chance to *reach!* Anything more is sheer nonsense and largely responsible for a great deal of mental anguish in our society today.

(17) Intuitiveness:

To be *really* good in the entrepreneurial world, I believe you must possess at least a moderately active sense of or feel for "things" and be willing to act on hunches in calculated risk situations. If you don't feel blessed in this regard that doesn't imply failure however.

(18) People:

You should be a good student of human behavior and have an acceptable track record of dealing with people and people problems. While there are numerous success stories of first class jackasses who couldn't have cared or known less about people, they are the exceptions. Hardly any skill will ultimately prove more valuable to you than the ability to know and deal with people!

(19) Capital Acquisition:

The entrepreneur must be able to raise, directly or indirectly, whatever capital is needed. Often times, failure to raise funds can be traced directly to an entrepreneur's simple aversion to this required task. You cannot be reticent or thin-skinned in this area. If your deal isn't good enough to "bother" a prospective investor or lender with, it isn't good enough for you to be bothered with either.

(20) Desire:

The dictionary defines desire as ''a strong feeling that impels to the attainment of something.'' In sports, they like to call it ''second effort.'' I believe that's all we need say ... except, you'll need plenty of it.

——— o ———

If you've completed this self-analysis with honesty and your overall assessment is on the low side of 5, perhaps all is not lost. It depends on your own specific set of circumstances. While clearly, I hope, you should not cast yourself in the role of head or sole entrepreneur, your idea may very well lend itself to a ''joint venture,'' so to say. For example, if you have already, or really know you can, come up with a prototype of a product or service, consider the possibility of associating with someone who *does* rate out highly in these entrepreneurial characteristics. It will probably be unrealistic for you to expect to be positioned as the majority shareholder in such an arrangment. But then, I'm not certain you ''deserve'' to be or need to be. The old saying of, ''I'd rather have X% of *something* than 100% of nothing'' may be appropriate. Because, if you aren't entrepreneurially talented, that's exactly what you could wind up with ... nothing.

Of course, another alternative (and a very excellent one indeed) is to go ahead and develop your idea to an extent that would make it interesting to, and possible for, a substantial and reputable company to buy the rights for your idea. If this appears to be the route for you, let me urge you to retain excellent legal counsel from the very beginning ... do not wait until you have everything ''all put together.''

So, we've come up with four alternatives relative to how you scored as a prospective entrepreneur. If you're high ... you can try it. If you're low ... you can drop it or acquire an entrepreneurial-type associate or produce a prototype in your garage in your leisure time and sell it to a corporation.

Perhaps the most subtle mistake people make in the decision to become an entrepreneur, as it pertains to whether or not they're qualified is:

21

(21) Genuine Interest In Business:

You have to like business-business, so to say. You should realize the simple fact that a business of your own means just that ... it is a *business* ... not an art shop, or machine shop, or electronics, or chemicals, or anything else.

I've purposely disassociated number 21 from the other criteria in order to dramatize the importance of it. Surprisingly (perhaps) a great many people in business for themselves do not like the *business* aspect of being in business. "If I could just make and fondle the product, I'd love what I do ... it's all this 'other stuff' that drags me down" is not an uncommon statement. That's ironic but it's true. It's also true, for the most part, that people who feel this way never seem to have very solid operations going. They just grind along doing about the same, year after year. I think this must be a slower "death" than any corporate situation.

THE EXPERIENTIAL FACTOR:

Because of the general nature of this book and the varying degree to which experience, per se, might be necessary to any given type of venture, it would serve little purpose to present a checklist of *mandatory* experience. And too, I subscribe to the proposition that basic managerial talent can be transferred from one industry to another.

Still, the general functions indigenous to any business, and those specific to your venture, must be served effectively, one way or the other, either through previous experience on your part (or your ability to quickly acquire skills) or the inclusion of experienced people in your operation.

Finally, if you possess the personal characteristics necessary for entrepreneurship, you'll be able to ascertain the level of experience required for your operation and how it will be supplied.

IV

PERSONAL PITFALLS

O.K., you've decided that you're venturing for the right reason(s) and you have the entrepreneurial credentials to do so. Let's get at the third reason why people fail in business. Instead of Personal Pitfalls, I could have most appropriately used the single word, Ambush!! Because that's the effect of these subtle and insidious "little" areas. In the first place you don't expect them, you've never contemplated them (at least fully) and then ... bang! There they are; climbing right up your back. And suddenly, your energy is re-directed from the operation to overcoming the surprises and dealing with them. Secondly, their timing is magnificently coordinated with your point of highest vulnerability ... when things are beginning to get tough. Many of these ambushes are, by themselves, only irritants or sub-shocks. But they seldom come one at a time ... almost always in groups. This is when they take their toll; and the toll can be awesome.

It is pretty well understood and accepted today that many problems in our personal and business (or career) lives stem directly from the fact we don't feel good about ourselves, about who we are. Self-worth ... self-esteem, call it what you will. But don't fail to see the significance of it relative to what you're considering doing. The psychological community tells us we must have four things in our lives to nourish and maintain a good feeling of self worth:

(1) Strokes

(2) Stimulation

(3) Structure

(4) Security

It is not the purpose of this book to speak authoritatively about mental health, per se. But if you're going to be (or already are) an entrepreneur, you must realize and believe it requires an extraordinary amount of self-esteem. Entrepreneurship is a fearful punisher of self-worth when things aren't going well; which is precisely the time one needs desperately to feel good about oneself! I am irrevocably convinced a feeling of low self-worth is the underlying and critical reason for a vast number of failures people have in business venturing.

As you think about what you're going to do (or may be doing), try and consider how these four immensely important factors (Strokes, Stimulation, Structure and Security) can be served, and thus, your self-esteem maintained at the happy, operational level so vital to success as an entrepreneur.

This chapter deals with a number of things that can happen to the individual entrepreneur which are capable of striking numbing blows to the ego; of subtly under-mining and perhaps even destroying the success you so vitally pursue.

(1) Friends & Acquaintances:

Especially in business, careers, etc., most of us put on our best face to our friends and acquaintances. That's part of the "American Way"; even if we aren't particularly successful, we'd like people to think we are. The real danger for the budding entrepreneur lies in the fact that his friends and acquaintances don't know who he *really* is.

We don't go 'round broadcasting our deepest fears, and frailties as such. In fact, it's human nature for most of us to present ourselves to our friends in the manner we feel is most pleasing to them (and flattering to us). Since we value the friendship, and thus put value on what we think the giver of that friendship wants or likes, we very often distort the real I. Sure, that isn't how it should be ... we all ought to try and be who we really are ... but that's how it is for most of us. Continually propagandizing ourselves all over the place. The point, as a practical matter, is ... *to the extent that you're other than you really are to friends, just be sure the advice that comes from them is filtered through your understanding that they may not understand.* (For example, friends could easily interpret extroverted behavior to mean you'd be a super salesman, when actually, you're rather shy and have a particular aversion to sales.)

It works the other way too. Your friends, of course, want you to like them as well. Everyone likes to be complimented. You will be complimented when you announce to friends that you're going to start your own business. "Hey, that's great, Charlie. I know you have everything it takes to be successful ... sounds like you have a great idea ... that really takes guts ... and I admire and envy you" and on and on and on. (Till you begin to wonder if you perhaps haven't aimed too low. I mean maybe tendering for control of General Motors would be more in keeping for a guy with your talents.) Just remember ... these people don't actually have the slightest idea what you're about ... you're their *friend,* man, and "if old Charlie wants to do thus and so, why I'm behind him 100%."

One of the surest ways for you to accurately evaluate the opinion of friends is to go ahead and make your announcement, listen to what they have to say ... then, ask them if they'd like to invest in your venture. If they're hesitant about investing, ask them why. If the first answer is the lack of funds, and you sort of know or suspect they could handle it if they wanted to, try this approach. "Look, Fred ... I value your judgment very highly. About business in general and me specifically. Can you see any aspect of this thing that doesn't "compute" or, more importantly, do you know of any weaknesses I may have that you feel would be a problem? You know, I could be overlooking something about myself because I'm so turned-on about this deal." Then sit back and *listen* ... *hear* what's being said ... or not said! If Fred is your friend, he'll tell you what he thinks, or most of what he thinks, on both scores. (Just be sure you filter it through your objective computer.) If Fred finds *no* fault with either the business per se or you ... Fred is either stupid or Fred isn't really your friend.

Friends, after a point, don't really give a damn! That's a strong statement. That's also true. And it's O.K. It's human nature and it's very real. Where this aspect of friendship detrimentally rears its head is when you start running into rough water. It's also the time when one very naturally turns to friends. You can expect time, sympathy, and offers to "help in any way" and, perhaps, lots of advice ... initially. As the hard times continue, you'll begin to notice some disinterest that usually takes the form of the friend being more aggressive than usual in controlling the topic of conversation. Which isn't going to be about your operation if he can help it. Somehow, you'll find that you aren't getting together as often, if for no other reason than by your own choosing. Because you'll discover yourself becoming very self-conscious about the situation. Your friend doesn't want to really get together either. He figures he can't, or won't, help you and he's compassionate in the sense that he probably doesn't want to put you on the spot. Besides, your friend has his problems and his life and he can't (he really can't) solve yours. And so, you become an object of pity or disdain and the terrible part for you is the realization of what has happened. It can be a real downer.

Friends derive some sort of "pleasure" out of seeing someone who's failing or floundering. Sound perverse? C'mon now! I'll be surprised if you never found it comforting to bask in the light of someone else's problem. You mean to say you never sat around with a mutual friend of the person who was experiencing difficulty, feeling and talking very knowingly about why, how, what you warned him about, what you suggested to him, etc., etc.? Of course you have ... if you're honest. Makes you feel a bit superior doesn't it? Takes away some of that early envy and sting that you felt when he had the lime light and a new, adventurous undertaking before him. And you were stuck in your same old place wishing you could "get it together."

It is true. The world does love a winner. But start to fail ... well, people don't like to be around "losers" ... right? I mean what can a loser do for them. And the fear is the loser may ask them to do something for him. You're no longer in the main stream of things. You're an outcast. And God help you if this isn't the first time you've tried. You're suddenly a ne'er do well. "Good ole Charlie ... poor devil, looks like he'll never make it."

Of course you don't *hear* these comments. You don't have to. You can feel it, and you can see it. Dinner invitations fall off. Those with whom you had comfortable passing exchanges in the club, are now a little too overt in their greetings and much less interested in you joining the group. You aren't included in this function or that outing. Your opinion is much less sought, if at all. You're standing still and the world soars on by.

It's a lonely and bitter feeling. And unless you're prepared by having either experienced it first hand, or by reading and understanding what I'm saying here, it can be a rude and stultifying experience that can adversely affect your performance.

Just remember, when the going gets heavy what's really at stake. *You* are at stake. Not them ... not your friends or your friendships. By the same token that you're "passed over lightly" in times of trouble, so will you be most other times. I mean, none of us sit around thinking for very long about the other fellow and his problems. Were it that we could be so lucky as to have others perpetually concerned about our well being. But that isn't life. The only way your friends and acquaintances can become a real problem is if you get the situation out of perspective and let them. And you "let them" by being shocked at their behavior and feeling that *they* are the ones for whom you perform. Remember, you perform for yourself. Nothing you do or don't do is going to affect their lives ... only yours!!

(2) Family:

If it isn't right at home, it's going to be tough, if not impossible, to handle the calling of the entrepreneur. (That assumes you want to remain reasonably happily married.) Before you get too serious about the "wild blue yonder," stop and take a good look at your wife's propensity and tolerance for risk, for uncertainty, for insecurity. Because this woman with whom you're living can either be a vital instrument in a successful venture or *the* underlying reason for failing. Don't kid yourself. They *are* just that important ... no question!!

If your wife is overtly concerned about security, then I'd advise you right now to give up any thought of being an entrepreneur. (Unless, of course, you can find a way to effectively satiate that need. And dreams of riches in the future is NOT the way to do it.)

Assuming you determine she has the spirit and tolerance for an entrepreneurial undertaking, make her a party to your plans early on (but only *after* you've got your fantasy/dream down to earth in the form of realistic possibility). Because she's in it with you. Aside from the economic risks, she'll be the one bearing the *direct* onslaught of your frustrations, your anger, and your disappointments as you wage your battle. All your moods will come directly home to roost. You won't have those pals from the old company around to conduct your career grumbling with, etc. And you won't want to be sharing all your problems with friends either. So ... who gets "it"? She does. Perhaps the best way to impart what I know and feel about this subject is to simply list some very important dos and don'ts regarding the good women:

Don't bitch and grumble all the time. Nothing destroys support and understanding any quicker.

Don't think for a moment that you are free to devote *all* your time to the business. To be sure, it's going to take a lot of twelve plus hour days and seven day weeks to make it. But, if you don't give her *anything* of yourself, pretty soon she's not going to have anything to support!

Don't plan on having her work in the business unless you're absolutely certain she's qualified in all respects and you *both* feel strongly that you'd do well working together.

Do make certain she understands the entire situation going in and that you keep her fairly well up to date. If you leave her in the dark, I can almost promise you she will, unwittingly (of course), "pick" a critical time to say or do the "wrong thing." She won't intend it, she'll feel badly about it, but the effect is the same. And it's not her fault ... it's yours.

Do plot out on your weekly and monthly Plan of Action, things to do with and for her. They don't have to be big things. Just little things that let her know she's still a woman and you care about her. A lunch a week isn't too much. A handful of those roadstand flowers every few days and dinner and a movie out once a week. There is time and a need for that. Not just for her ... but for you, as well!

Do plan to just take a whole day off once in a while in the middle of the week. You can do it. If your deal is so shaky that you can't enjoy something like this occasionally, you're in deep trouble anyway and ought to be thinking about bailing out of there.

Do be very cautious about using your wife's money. That isn't to say it's a *bad* thing to do. But, I would urge you to take note of the following points:

(a) Don't plan to use *all* she has.

(b) Make a formal, written presentation to her just as you would any other investor. Be certain that she fully understands the situation. Do *not* accept a declaration of love and complete trust as a substitute.

(c) Evidence her investment in some formal, legal way.

(d) Be as sure as you can in your own mind you're not going to develop ego problems if things go bad and the money is lost.

(e) Be able to view her, and her money, just as you would view any investor. Being up-tight will cloud judgment and force errors.

Do have your wife read this book. Make sure she understands what it takes from you.

Before we leave the family, just a word about children. Before I had them, I knew all about them. Now, with three teenagers, I don't know a damn thing. But, I suggest you can't totally ignore them in terms of some of the decisions you will have to make and the effect it can have on *both* of you. Even the best adjusted person in their teens hates to move away from friends, is "frightened" by dad-the-dreamer, and the uncertainty that can accompany an entrepreneurial venture. Don't expect the teenager to be particularly sympathetic, especially if your plans affect him in any substantial way. They couldn't care less that you're going about self-actualizing your life. (Hell, that's what they think they're doing.) To them, you're good old "stable" dad ... already a winner or a loser, depending on (his) values, etc. I would suggest you attenuate the trauma from this quarter by writing a letter to your teenagers telling them what you're about and why. Let them know you're still very much involved in living *your* life. Ask for their understanding. And then put the matter behind

29

you. Don't let their problems be your problems in the sense that you become traumatized with guilt and worry about the effect your actions are having. If you make the judgment that what your children want is more important than what you want to do, it's no contest. Don't "do your thing!"

(3) The Ostrich Syndrome:

Some of the biggest failures people have made in business are a direct result of *refusing* to look at one or more important aspects of the venture. I know this sounds crazy, but it's absolutely true. Often the brightest people make this mistake. They almost purposely avoid a thorough investigation of some vital component. Let's take marketing. You've got a product, it's great, the profit margin is remarkable, even with generous over-budgeting on the expense side. Competition appears minimal and disorganized and you have proof that people or companies will purchase. You can produce the product or service with no problems. That's all you need to know, from the marketing point of view, so off you go.

Some months later, you discover that competition is broader than you thought, the market vastly smaller, and your product is no big deal with them because they've bought from your competition for years. Now how in the hell does that happen??? All the facts were there for you to see. And you're not stupid ... you know how to do basic market research. Well, I think I know what goes on in a situation like this. I know because it has happened to me.

First of all, you get excited when you have an idea. The thing that excites you is just that ... it's *your* idea! Nobody else knows. And you're secretive about it. So you begin to quietly probe here and there, careful not to arouse suspicion lest somebody steal your idea (or improve their deal with your idea). You're gonna spring it on the world ... right? Well, if you're *too* careful, it could spring right back in your face.

The other aspect of the matter is the *fragility* of an idea. It is so fragile when it first comes. Be careful lest someone put it down. It's so easy to become discouraged with that new infant of promise and glory. It needs to get strong before it's exposed to the harsh light of the world. And you know what happens ... sometimes? You purposely don't turn the next page or make twenty more phone calls or see a few more people, etc. You don't want to risk discouragement because it *is* a good deal. You really don't want to dig all the way because you're afraid you'll find out it's *not* such a good deal after all.

And the insanity of it all is that you sorta realize what you're doing while you're doing it. Down deep you do. But you just stumble on out there hoping, I guess.

The very best time and money you'll ever spend in any potential project is the research you do before committing. Dig till you're absolutely certain that you've covered every conceivable aspect that you know how to cover. I promise you ... if a deal is a good one, you won't lose or destroy it by completely researching it. If it doesn't stand up then ... it never would have in actual operation.

Don't be discouraged when you find that your idea isn't novel. There is nothing really *new* in this world. You've heard that before and it's true. There are just little "eighths-of-a-turn," a hair's breadth here and there, that make the difference ... that make something "new." That's what we're all looking for.

(4) Your Personal Credit & Reputation:

I was three or four months into my first venture before I encountered this little area of rude reality. I had been a banker in a large city and had done well. It was necessary for me to spend a couple of months in another city in the early going of my new company. One afternoon, I stopped by a clothing store to pick up some shirts. As I paid for them, I was invited to open a charge account. Why not? I'd be there for a while and, after that, in and out a good deal. It would be convenient.

Later that evening, I sat down to complete the application. Question 4 or 5, Employer? I proudly wrote down ... self-employed. Next question, How Long? It was a little uncomfortable, but I cheated and wrote down ... two months. Two weeks later, I received a polite and apologetic note to the effect that I didn't meet the requirements for credit. Whereupon I stormed down to that little store and demanded to know if they knew to whom they were denying credit. They said they did. A self-employed fellow of two months. Now that got my attention!

I had no idea that for many years I'd been introducing myself and obtaining credit "under the name of my company." When I said I'm so and so with the bank or filled out a credit application with the bank as my employer what I was really saying was, "I'm the Bank!!"

It comes as a rather unpleasant and ego-deflating shock to discover that you're really "nothing" economically speaking ... by yourself. It took me about two or three weeks to get over that one. And even today, there are still "problems." It still "bugs" me and I'm still a bit defensive about it.

But here are a couple of ways to cope. Before you ever leave the corporate nest, make sure you have all the credit cards and charge accounts you can get. Secondly, if it looks as if you'll need to finance a new car or a house or additonal life and disability insurance, do it now. Thirdly, never write "self-employed" on any application. Simply put the name of your company in that blank. You're not trying to be evasive or dishonest; you're going to pay your bills. What you're doing is giving the grantor of the credit you seek a better chance to do business with you.

Buying a home can be an especially tough proposition at a time when you may be strapped for operating cash in the company and looking for as small a down payment as possible. You should be aware of the fact that the lender is going to want to see your last three years' tax returns and (maybe) the financial statements of your company for the same period. (Often times, your best route may be assumption.)

Just be aware of these things and don't let them throw you into a funk. Two other quick thoughts. It might be worth talking with some other "self-employed" to see how they manage. And, you should always discuss your personal financial needs or intentions with your banker.

(5) The "Gut" Feel:

I'm going to assume you have a higher active intuitiveness than the average man on the street. I'm not certain how much good it will do to tell you that most of the big mistakes I've made have been because I didn't follow my instincts. Sometimes the gut can mislead you to be sure. But I believe the vast majority of the time you should listen to that "little voice." I am *not* suggesting facts are unimportant. They're critical of course. But once you've got the reasonably obtainable "facts," follow your best instincts. You can't nor should you try, to quantify everything. Quantitative analysis can take you just so far ... too much can result in inaction and indecision and those two can be deadly. You can always find reasons *not* to do something or why something won't work.

(6) Getting Back In:

The first time you'll usually be confronted with the thought of "getting back in" is when things really get tough for the first, or maybe the second, time. This is when you begin doubting the venture is going to succeed and, as a hedge, start to look around. You drop a hint to a couple of friends and chat with a head-hunter or two. And your feed back is sorta zero. If it comes as a surprise to you at this critical time of trouble in the business, three bad things can happen. You get even more despondent and your performance with your operation will suffer. Secondly, you could make such a panic induced assault on the job market that you do all the wrong things and produce nothing (and that's an excellent way to get word around town that you're in trouble with the business). Finally, you could be driven further into the entrepreneurial area in the sense that you give up hope of ever being employable again (as you'd like to be). And this comes at a time when your self-confidence is almost non-existent, funds probably pretty close to being exhausted and you may have found out, but not recognized quite yet, that you really aren't entrepreneurial material. The only word that fits this situation is (potential) disaster.

The secret again is knowing what *can* happen in this area. And if you see it coming you can deal with it successfully, now that you understand it.

Experience indicates the better way to deal with this situation is, for openers, to stay very, very cool. Take a few days off to think things through. Then, if your decision is to get back in, I would suggest:

(a) Do *not* disband your venture overnight. At least plan to keep the shell alive. What you need is an employment base from which to re-enter.

(b) If at all possible, retain an office facility.

(c) Seek professional assistance, either directly or from some excellent books now on the market.

33

(d) For at least some period of time, it will be advantageous to assume the posture that, while your company is not making you as wealthy as you had hoped, you're doing O.K. You can also add the thought that your venture has become totally unchallenging and unrewarding. The "action" is slow and you're bored by responsibilities beneath your level of competence. In other words, you're underemployed.

(e) When it's time to say you've failed, do so in a positive manner. *Be proud of the effort you made* ... not negative and apologetic about the failure. Most of all, don't blame others ... business associates, vendors, customers, etc., etc. In mentioning others, it's probably best to simply say nothing.

(7) Faith, Pride, and Knowing When to Cut Losses:

Above all, you must maintain both faith and pride in your product (or service) and yourself. Probably the earliest indication that these two vital areas are running into trouble is when you respond to the question, "what do you do" with a "downer" on whatever it is you do. In other words, when you find yourself apologizing for it, attempting to evade the question, hoping the question won't be asked, feeling what you do is not as substantive as something someone else does, taking 15 minutes to offer an unnecessary and unrequested detailed explanation, etc.

Another excellent indicator is when you find yourself giving up too easily on a sales call or not pursuing a critical financing problem past the first banker that says no. When you're no longer willing to go that last mile because you *"know* it's gonna work out if you just persevere."* Now ... RIGHT NOW ... is the time to bring yourself up short. Take two or three days, a week, whatever, and get away. Try to let things sort of settle and rethink what has happened. There's only one thing worse than failing and that's to *continue* failing in any given venture.

To be certain, you don't want to go off and leave something good on the table, as they say. But, I've got a better saying ... you know for certain what's left in your pocket and, at this stage, it's hard to go wrong with cash.

So, unless there are extenuating circumstances such as fatigue, personal problems, anything along these lines that caused you to "slump," that you can *positively identify* as such, the time to cut your losses and get the hell out is NOW. There's a great big difference between a quitter and a smart businessman.

(8) Business Associates:

I'm speaking specifically about the person(s) with whom you're involved in the direct conduct of the business. Partner(s) and/or shareholder(s). These people should come under the closest possible scrutiny. It's almost always fatal if you and your associate(s) have a "falling out."

In the beginning, when you're excited and anxious, it's easy not to question this area too closely. I mean you wouldn't even be considering a business relationship if "he" was a bad guy. So, he has passed the "first test" already. And, as you move along in your plans, you'll have an opportunity to observe. That may, however, not be a good enough test. In fact, I hope you will assume that it isn't and take the additional step of checking with your proposed associate's former associates. What you'll be looking for is one of two responses on the negative side. Usually, if a man has some sort of *real* problem, a former associate will come right out with it. Or, he'll be so vague and non-committal that you'll know something is very wrong somewhere. Either response deserves whatever further investigation is possible. If you determine that he does have a significant problem, my advice is to forget the deal. At the very least, you should not go forward in an equal ownership (or control) situation.

The greatest errors in judgment you can make in attempting to configure the deal so you can "live with" what you perceive may be a difficult individual are:

(a) Attempting to contract, or otherwise legally agree, the problem into oblivion. It can't be done. The personality always transcends the document.

(b) Thinking your ability to deal with problems of human behavior will triumph. That's suicidal. Ask a psychiatrist, for example, how you deal with a paranoid personality. If he's honest, his answer will probably be, "you don't."

(c) Letting hope for gain in the long run overshadow the reality of the short run. The short-run is where you make it or lose it. And this is precisely where any abnormal problems with an associate will take their greatest toll. I'm suggesting the wrong choice of a business associate almost automatically precludes success.

What happens if you're unable to discern an associate problem going in, but three months later you're wondering if it's worth it? The odds are overwhelming that you're right; it isn't going to be worth it. Trying to simply ignore the problem is the worst mistake you can make at this stage. Deal with it one way or the other ... now! I think you have two logical choices:

(a) If you want to make a further effort, figure out exactly how you're going to do it; then, set a *time limit* for positive results and *stick to it*.

(b) Get out now.

There are, I'm sure, extenuating circumstances, in some instances, that would justify ignoring a serious problem of a prospective associate. It's just that *I* don't know what they'd be.

Regardless of what kind of business associates you may have, good communications are an absolute must! And a substantial part of your communication should be (ultimately) reduced to writing. This not only goes a long way in preventing problems but, if and when they arise ... there it is in black and white.

(9) Books:

They can be remarkably helpful and incredibly misleading and detrimental. I say "they" can. What I mean, of course, is the way in which people use them. For our purposes here, let's divide the "book world" into two categories. The "How" books ... How To, How I Did, How You Can, etc. The second group, we'll refer to as the "Technical" books, e.g., text, reference, "hand" books, etc.

(a) The "How" Books:

These are the ones to be particularly careful of. They can "turn you on" through over-simplification ... cause you to ignore or be oblivious of three very important factors:

36

(1) About 99% of the hard work, trials and tribulations in- volved in an enterprise.

(2) The all important factor of timing, especially, as to the marketing proposition, e.g., state of the economy, de- mand, costs, availability, competition, etc.

(3) The personality and acumen of the original "doer."

In other words, the success was a result of a lot of hard work, at precisely the right time, by somebody who really knew what the hell he was doing and/or was "lucky." The watch-phrase is simple . . . Don't Try to *Duplicate!* Use these books as interesting references at best.

(b) The "Technical" Books:

Two important thoughts about books in this category. First, don't expect to ever find a book that is 100% applicable to what you're trying to do. Innovation and revision will al- ways be necessary for productive application to your ven- ture. These books must be adapted to consider your own special requirements. Yes, I'll agree that what I've just said is basic common sense. The thing that bothers me is, it isn't uncommon to see situations where someone has pre- cisely "slaved" to the text. Secondly, always relate the date of publication and the authors credentials to the situation with which you're dealing.

An excellent method of locating the best available books on any given subject is ask the professionals in that field; which includes the academic community, syndicated columnists and other non-practicing specialists.

The intent of this "Books" section is not to make a case *against* the use of books or, in any way, depreciate the value thereof. My case is simply against the *mis-use* of what otherwise can be of immense help to you. The value of any book, in the final analysis, is in direct proportion to (a) how much you need the data (b) how well you can absorb and relate the data and (c) how available that data is elsewhere.

37

In any event, books can and should fill *only a part* of the basic research and guidance necessary for the evolvement and operation of a venture.

(10) Loneliness & Aloneness:

The two loneliest places in the world are at the very top of any organization and being an entrepreneur. Thus, you should be certain that keeping your own council is comfortable for you. For example, if you enjoy spending a portion of each day in your corporate life "jawing" with associates about problems, office politics, etc., this may be an excellent indicator that you could have some real problems when there's no one to talk to! You should have the capacity for being alone. Which, in part, means that it's stimulating, challenging, and productive. A moment ago, we talked about liking one's self. If it's just you, you better be friendly.

Being alone and being lonely are not the same, of course, I've found that loneliness sets in when anxiety increases and hope decreases. And it's a very short and quick slide from loneliness to despondency to depression. If you hang around any of these "stops" too long, you may very well derail that train to success.

The answer that works for me, and will for you, is the recognition and acceptance that you *will* experience loneliness and the resulting moods. But knowing this before it occurs allows you the edge you need to reduce the trauma to an acceptable level. The acceptable level is not permitting it to render you ineffective at the wrong time or for any sustained length of time.

During a period of loneliness or depression, the business always looks its worst and personal relationships always suffer the most. Incentive drops to zero. And, it's very possible to so project yourself out of the venture that's "causing you" to feel miserable, you sometimes are never able to get back in it. These are the "hang tough" periods. The inability to effectively anticipate and handle these periods can be found at the roots of a significant number of unsuccessful entrepreneurial efforts.

(11) The Corporate Syndrome:

If you're in at least middle management of a corporation, and have never been on your own before, you have no idea how much is done *for* you. Perhaps, you'll respond by saying you have X people with X titles and X responsibilities at your beck and call. But, do you really know WHAT and HOW they do? Chances are you don't. You either have never known or you've forgotten. And I'm almost positive your hand never held a (corporate) broom or brewed the daily coffee.

This is another of those surprise areas that can and will, if you aren't careful, make you crazy. Face it, you're not an executive any longer in the sense that you ''simply'' conceive, decide and delegate. You are now the Commander AND the Commandee. Compared to the ship's captain, the lowly garbage dumper aboard a vessel isn't too important. But if that garbage doesn't go over the side, you can't believe how important that dumper is going to become in about a week to ten days!

What happens to many people when they're suddenly confronted with all the mundaneness of mass minutia is an overreaction (a) *financially* by overstaffing (b) *egotistically* by feeling they're above it all (c) *emotionally* by getting angry and not attending to matters. Any or all three of these situations are, to say the least, not good for the venture. Again, attention is diverted and energy mis-spent. Reconcile yourself to a realistic level of functioning as a jack-of-all trades.

Conversely, I will be very quick to add the all important other side of the coin. Gross *under*staffing presents an even more serious potential for emotional chaos and thus impairment of a venture. If there's a secret to heading off this ambush, it's knowing *your* specific value to the venture and making certain your plans permit adequate application of that value! If your financial projections can't afford the manifestation of your talent, you can't afford the venture. If you discover somewhere down the line you've erred in this regard, you should immediately stop and try to formulate a correction. If no way can be found to relieve the situation, serious thought should then be given to abandoning the project.

(12) Murphy's Law:

''WHATEVER CAN GO WRONG...WILL!!'' Surely everyone is aware of Mr. Murphy. But, it probably finds its sublime manifestation in the entrepreneurial venture. You can get pretty paranoid pretty quickly if you're not careful. The best advice I can offer in combatting emotional trauma and rendering Murphy as harmless as possible is to suggest you develop a (healthy) sense of humor about him. You just have to be able to laugh it off and go on. If you take this phenomenon too seriously, you'll wind up spending all your time chasing the unimportant phantom of perfection. And in the end, he'll haunt you to failure.

Just be totally assured, regardless of how well you plan, things will not happen per se as you plan. The danger lies in not recognizing or accepting this fact and getting down on yourself.

(13) Preparation of Self:

This is most often a problem where the budding entrepreneur is changing fields entirely (or taking on the *overall* aspect of an operation for the first time). It's the former instance where fantasy can really obliterate us. It isn't that we aren't aware we'll have to learn. It's because we can seriously misjudge how *extensive* a new role really is and the amount of time required to reach an operationally productive level. "Well, hell, I can do that," has been the downfall of a lot of good people. Sure... you are, I am, everybody is, "different"... we're all unique. But most of us also share the uniqueness of not being able to do something new any (or a whole lot) sooner or better than anyone else. To be sure, there are many exceptions to my point. But, my point is still valid. There has to be a reason why even the very best professionals in any field continually pursue knowledge in that field. It's simple... the further one goes into something, the more he finds there is to find. What the person changing fields needs to ascertain is:

(a) The (known) breadth and depth of the field.

(b) The realistic time factor it will take (him) to become *productive*.

(c) Will he really like what he is seeking upon full exposure to it.

I believe the seriousness of changing fields is fully worth the consideration of removing the "will I like it, can I do it" risk. What I'm suggesting then is taking a "preliminary apprenticeship." This can be done by putting together some vacation plus some leave for personal reasons, etc. Often, four straight weeks of total involvement with something new will be enough to at least true your perspective.

Again and again, inadequately prepared people venture forth into some new field only to find that they've fallen prey to fantasy. Four weeks or so is an exceedingly cheap price to pay. I hope you'll see the wisdom of the purchase.

(14) Perseverance:

If you can use any one word to define the secret or key to success, this is it. If you have a *viable* project and you're able to persevere, you'll succeed. When you really think about it, I believe you'll agree. Not one problem we've discussed, or will discuss, is really insurmountable if you have the capacity and toughness to persevere. Neither education nor talent nor intelligence can replace it. All of the failure inducing aspects of this chapter begin their effectiveness via the erosion of an individual's perseverance.

A word of caution. Perseverance does not imply dogmatism. An extremely important factor in (productive) perseverance is *flexibility*. Failure to distinguish the difference between the need to (a) push on as originally planned and (b) back away, regroup and take a different approach, can easily destroy your venture! Knowing *where* that point is is highly judgmental and quanti-resistant. The best assistance in "knowing" probably comes in the form of two words . . . suspicion and inquiry. The first inkling you have that something isn't right, stop and question "what's going on"; which should include seeking the judgment of others.

(15) Money:

Failure to realistically understand and acknowledge the importance of money, in all its aspects, will get you into more trouble than you ever dreamed existed. It's uncanny how many people choke to business death on this seemingly obvious fact.

Three specific mistakes people most commonly make about money in a personal sense are:

(a) Believing they can successfully handle a personal budget that has been *drastically* reduced in order to make the business effort.

(b) Counting on too high a draw from the company, especially in the early going.

41

(c) Beginning to "live it up" too soon in terms of expensive cars, boats, jewelry, vacations, etc.

All three of the above are capable of creating major trauma; diverting attention and energy away from the enterprise.

Perhaps, the most damaging of these three is trying to live on less than you're emotionally geared to live on. I don't think there's any damn virtue at all in personal financial chaos. Instead of having the effect of really making you work hard, it'll drag you down to the point of perhaps saying to hell with it all. Starting you own company doesn't imply poverty conditions any more than it does instant wealth. Make sure there are provisions for whatever it is you need.

As far as living it up too soon is concerned, I don't have a lot of patience with this problem. I almost feel as if the person who does this deserves what happens. On the other hand, I'd offer this one suggestion. Look eighteen to twenty-four months ahead and see what your company's financial situation would look like if your current projections turn out to be 50% worse than anticipated. Then, adjust your pro forma earnings accordingly and consider spending half the net income of that picture. (But only after you've had a session with your tax advisor.) Don't misunderstand what I'm saying. I think it's quite acceptable to prudently and gradually increase your "take" in whatever form (salary, auto, etc.) is desirable as you go along. It's the jump from VW to Rolls that kills.

(16) The Business Plan:

In sophisticated financial circles, the formal Business Plan is a proposal submitted to potential equity investors. It categorically and systematically sets out every vital aspect of the venture and projects results out through five years. It is a comprehensive and detailed view of the enterprise. The pertinence of the Business Plan in this chapter is what the *absence* of one can do.

The majority of people who fail in business begin with start-up situations on money secured from friends and relatives. Thus, they are not "forced" to prepare a Business Plan as such. Even though your "lay" investors don't require one, *you* ought to require one. It is an excellent, and I believe mandatory, "exercise" that will bring whatever you're trying to do together for you. Looking back on failure, most people will acknowledge they probably wouldn't have even made the attempt if they had done in-depth planning.

On the other hand, there will be far fewer "Oh, hell, I never thought about *that*" sort of situations which, when you stop to think about it, always have trouble as their base! You know yourself you never feel any more inadequate and depressed than when you realize you've made a "dumb" and unnecessary mistake. And the realization that good planning could have prevented this or that really makes you feel like a total incompetent. The last place you need to feel that way is in the midst of running your own business. You'll be well served to construct a Business Plan for your venture along the lines of the example in the back of this book.

(17) Time:

There is a studied redundancy in this book regarding TIME. No other single factor is so elusive and so potentially disastrous as the miscalculation of time. This is true because:

(a) "It" almost always takes longer than you anticipated, regardless of the function or undertaking involved.

(b) Since time costs you nothing *initially,* it's the easiest aspect of the venture to manipulate in your projections.

(c) In the initial stages of anything, hopes are always highest; thus, the tendency to be overconfident about how long it will take you and/or others to accomplish any given task or project.

(d) Your economics are invariably tied directly to time.

Obviously the best way to deal with this situation and not permit yourself to be caught in a crippling time bind is to plan realistically and formally (see Plan of Action in Chapter VIII). You can't believe how terribly destructive time problems can be to your self-esteem. You may never feel so inadequate or helpless. Whatever is missed or does not occur on schedule coupled with the "shock" of error puts thousands of entrepreneurs into deep trouble every year.

(18) The Salesman(?):

Failure to realistically distinguish between sales and marketing, *relative to your involvement,* could cost you your venture! If you're now, or ever have been, a salesman, you will have little or no problem with this pitfall. If not, look out! Here's what can happen.

Our old friend fantasy jumps up again and co-mingles the two words sales and marketing via the excitement that accompanies figuring out all the ways and means to move your product or service. How you're going to do it ... that's MARKETING. And marketing is an EXECUTIVE function ... one you're accustomed to. And there we have the trap!

You don't have any experience that tells you whether you *can* sell, whether you *like* to sell or even have the capacity to successfully *tolerate* sales.

Try and imagine the intense and debilitating shock that comes, a few months into the venture, with the discovery that (a) you absolutely detest selling and (b) the only way your venture is going to succeed is if you perform as a top-notch salesman!

It isn't a question of whether or not you *can* sell; of course you can sell . . . any of us *can* sell. The issue is *will* you sell . . . or is selling so repugnant your efforts to avoid it will result in trauma deep enough to undermine the entire venture!

Some people just hate sales. It's that simple. But, as president of your operation, you're going to *have* to sell! I don't care what kind of undertaking is involved, the *president* has to sell, to one degree or another, because he is the president!

It will be helpful to you in pondering your own reaction to the thought of being a salesman to consider sales in two extremes. First, *executive* selling wherein you're calling on high level executives in substantial corporations whom you either know or have solid introductions to. The second situation involves *cold calling* on small companies where the sale is made to unsophisticated people, low on the totem pole and the sales pitch delivered on the floor of the business in full sight and sound of customers, fellow employees, etc.

The message, I hope, is simple. *Know* what it's going to take to sell and be certain you're not placing a responsibility on yourself you won't be able to handle.

V

FINANCING THE VENTURE

Putting all else aside, money is what it's all about. Your ability to get money and earn money is the realistic difference between success and failure in business. Make a mistake about this and you can be dead. As a former flight instructor once said to our class, "If we can hook up enough power to this building we're in, we can fly it." So it is with business and money. If there's enough money (and you're "good" and have a viable idea), your business will be successful. An over-statement? Perhaps . . . but any "overage" is nit-picking.

So much time and effort is wasted, not to mention money, by people who are convinced the world is waiting for their product or service (and investors and lenders are waiting with funds) they completely ignore the reality of money! If I can just persuade you to believe there is *no substitute* for money, I will have done you a great service. This statement however does not detract one iota from the proposition that if you have a viable idea and the entrepreneurial talent to pursue it, you will eventually be successful. It does, in fact, *support* it! All the stories we hear about people with no money, struggling and finally breaking through to success are true. But, part of that struggle was *for money!* Sooner or later, in one form or another, they broke through, so to say, with *money!*

The purpose of this chapter is not to present the ABC's of finance. There are many excellent publications that provide this data. What I want to impart are some *practical* views concerning the subject of finance; thoughts with which to over-lay the ABC's and your own particular situation. Most of the self-help or how-to things I read about the financial aspects of business, seem to approach the subject as if understanding the ABC's of finance somehow guarantees the availability of funds as well as your ability to obtain them.

There are as many "ways" to finance a business venture as there are business ventures. And each one is a little different. So it's impossible for anyone to give you a set pattern to follow . . . at least one that's truly viable. What this means is, *you* are going to have to develop your own financial equation. To be sure, I'll have some suggestions and we'll talk about the more obvious sources of money, etc. But after you've done all your reading and talking, you'll be the final architect. And the soundness of your financial design will (probably) determine success or failure.

ILLUSIONS OF SUCCESS:

From time to time, we all see situations that cause us to wonder *how* some people "do it." Their background and basic operation simply does not give very clear evidence as to how it all came about. Haven't you, at least once, listened to someone tell a story about another person's success and mentally scratched your head thinking, "damn, I must really be inadequate." Or at least, "well, if that clown can do that, I certainly can. I'm in the wrong business." Friends, there's a whole lot we can't and don't see in situations like this. Just recently, I admired the most fashionable and palatial home in a small lake resort community. I was told the owner ran the X hamburger franchise in the small town near by. Well, that didn't sound "just right." Further inquiry noted that he owned *nineteen* of these franchises in as many little towns in a radius of some one hundred miles. Now that makes a little more sense. But, how do you get to own nineteen franchises? I'd met the owner some weeks back and he didn't impress me as someone who could put together an operation that was (reportedly) netting him around $25,000 per month before taxes. The more I thought about it the more curious I became and, finally, I went by to see him. When I left some two hours later, I had nothing but sheer envy in place of my original wonderment. Behind it all was the sale, some four years earlier, of 500 acres of land his father had left him over thirty years before that. He'd sold to developers at $3,000 per acre.

There is so much money available to so many people from private and undisclosed "personal" sources that it is very easy for those of us with none to be misled by someone else's "seeming" success. I find that most people are extremely reluctant to ever admit or disclose:

(a) Their financial backing came from "family funds," whether it be from family inheritance per se, or in the form of a wife's "dowry."

(b) The fact that if the money *was* theirs and the venture failed, all would not be lost because there was family money, in *some* form, upon which to fall back in order to survive economically.

(c) They were the recipient of the wealth, ability, generosity and confidence of a successful mentor. A "great white father," if you will.

Another excellent example, to drive home my point, is a recent discussion I had with a good friend involving whether I wanted to become involved in an unusually high-risk venture. When I expressed some reluctance, my friend chided, "Why, I thought you were in the business of taking risks?"

"Frank," I said, "if this deal completely blows . . . I mean we lose *everything* we put in, isn't it a fact that you and Carol will continue to live in your present (half-million dollar) home, drive your four expensive cars, recreate at your two second homes, send your children to private schools, and have ample funds with which to begin again?"

"Well," he somewhat heatedly replied, "What the hell does that have to do with anything? . . . I still lose just as much as you do!"

"You really believe that's the measure don't you, Frank?"

"Absolutely," he replied.

With that, I just smiled and said I'd see him around.

If you don't have anything except what *you're* capable of producing, your dreams and subsequent plans must recognize that fact. Don't do your thinking and planning in the Judas light of, "because he or they did it, I've got the *same* chance and I'll do it." If your plans are fused in the crucible of your own reality and the project is still viable, you've got a good chance.

FINANCIAL REALITIES:

Now, let's look at a few hard realities concerning money as it relates to the business venture.

(1) Money, sufficient cash and credit, is absolutely essential if you're going to succeed. It's simply amazing how many people, who would subscribe 100% to this obvious statement, go right ahead *knowing* they don't have funds enough to even reach the point where they have a chance to supplement cash-flow needs. If you're going out desperately under-capitalized, hoping for a miracle, at least put a time limit on the miracle. That way, you pre-plan an intelligent shut-down point that guarantees you'll eat beyond the folly. The point of shut down should be either when you get down to a minimum of four months personal budget or have a job waiting when you run out of cash.

(2) It is extremely difficult to raise any *substantial* amount of money for a start-up situation, unless you are fortunate enough to count yourself, in one (or more) of the following categories:

(a) You are a highly respected and well-known executive venturing in your own field of expertise.

(b) You happen to have an exceptional idea in an industry that is "hot."

(c) You've been able to cultivate someone of wealth who respects your abilities and judgment.

(d) You're a veritable master of persuasion and are lucky.

(3) The "average" person with an "average" idea is realistically limited to the amount of money and credit he can raise from his own assets, friends, relatives and whatever trade credit he may be able to arrange.

(4) Undercapitalization is an exercise in how little you can lose as opposed to how much you can make.

EQUITY CAPITAL OR WORKING CAPITAL:

Semantics can sometimes present annoying problems in financial discussions. Worse yet, they can be responsible for a great deal of wasted time and effort in the putting together of a deal. So, I think it will be time well spent to briefly review some definitions.

Everyone knows the difference between the two basic types of capital used in business, right? *Equity* and *Working* capital. But do you really? Let's say you have firm purchase orders from a Fortune 500 company of impeccable financial strength and you need $50,000 to lay in additional equipment and manpower to fill those orders. Are you looking for Equity capital or Working capital? The answer (most probably) is, it depends upon whom you're asking. If it's a commercial bank, they may tell you you're looking for Equity money (and they only supply Working capital)! The problem of differentiation is intensified sometimes by the use of words other than "equity" and "working."

What I want to do here is:

(a) Make you aware that problems can arise from not properly understanding what these terms mean.

(b) Urge you to never be hesitant to ask what is meant by a word or term used in connection with finance that you don't *fully* understand.

(c) Functionally or classically differentiate between the terms Equity Capital and Working Capital.

Working Capital: Funds that are used to perform the work of the business. The *excess* of current assets over current liabilities. If there is no excess, funds may be borrowed from various commercial lenders. What the lender is doing is substituting *cash,* needed now, for current assets that have value but no current liquidity. The borrowed funds are then repayable to the lender as those current non-liquid assets are eventually converted to cash, e.g., when an account receivable is paid.

Equity Capital: Funds used to start-up or purchase or expand a business that represent the value or worth of that business. In a start-up situation, funds that come from the *owners* of the business and/or non-commercial sources such as friends and relatives. These funds are not repayable.

CASH FLOW:

I've chosen to highlight the subject of cash flow in a separate section because of its extreme importance in the financial equation.

When the average person sits down to begin figuring what his idea looks like in terms of dollars and cents, his first step is to estimate income and expense, first on an annual basis. If his figures show a profit, then he gets a little more serious and breaks the year down into months. What he has prepared, of course, is a Profit & Loss statement. Many people think that's enough, and they plunge right on in ... only to find some three or four months later they have no available cash! The information you must have about your cash availability or cash flow is not available from the (typical) P&L statement.

A cash flow schedule or statement, as the name implies, tells you how much cash you will need, when you'll need it, and where it will come from. It is prepared from, or in conjunction with, your P&L and has the effect of telling you whether your P&L (your deal, actually) is a financial *possibility.*

The significance of preparing and maintaining a cash flow projection will be immediately obvious from a simple examination of the format itself (see back of book).

THE BUSINESS PLAN & THE LOAN PACKAGE:

When you blow all the "smoke" away, what both of these compilations do is describe your deal. The essential differences between a Business Plan and a Loan Package is that the former is more extensive and, as we noted in Chapter III, used to present a deal to sophisticated professional equity investors. The Loan Package, as the name implies, is utilized in the acquisition of a loan.

While many lenders and some lay investors may not require a formal presentation as such, sooner or later they will want most of the information contained in one. What happens is, they'll ask for this and that and the other as you "work your way through" the acquisition of funds process. Thus, it makes sense to go ahead and "pull your deal" together on paper before you start making the rounds.

Of course, if you've approached the possibility of your venture in an intelligent manner, you already *have* a Business Plan or Loan Package of sorts. All you need do, probably, is arrange your data in a format preferred by financial people. For this purpose, I've included a more or less standard Business Plan for you to follow. I suggest you not worry about a Loan Package, as such, until a lender tells you your Business Plan will not suffice and provides a specific form for his requirements.

Business Plans and Loan Packages are most often thought of as a "sales brochure" for the purpose of selling your deal to an investor or lender. I like to think of them exactly in reverse; as a tool to *sell myself* on the financial feasibility of what I'm proposing. I hope you'll be persuaded to take the same view.

THE START-UP:

I think most knowledgeable people will agree that a going concern is the better way, all other things being equal, to go into business. The problem is finding a clean, reasonably priced company to buy. Thus, most people must start their own operation "from scratch."

There was some temptation to employ the case study method in dealing with this section. But, I've concluded what I want to impart can be more easily and effectively assimilated and utilized in narrative form. The application of the following data to your own specific proposition should prove far more helpful than attempting to mold your proposed venture to some model I might create consisting of financial statement exhibits, footnotes, explanations, etc.

The following observations are both a result of how I personally have "found things to be" as well as what concerns many others who come to me for advice. Had I understood and *applied* the data you're about to review, early in my entrepreneurial career, my "rearing," as it were, would have been far less painful.

(1) Divide the evolvement of your operation into stages. This permits you to more accurately and clearly define financial needs in terms of time which, in turn, will dictate ways and means to finance the venture.

(a) Gearing-Up: This phase should include all costs and activities from organization of the venture through the completion and testing of a prototype of a product or service.

(b) Bridging: Depending on the type of business, there can often be a lull between completion of the first stage and the beginning of full operational status. For example, you may need a certain period of time to negotiate and consummate sales agreements, lay in and "de-bug" equipment, conclude additional financing, etc. This can be an extremely critical period and many ventures succumb because the entrepreneur fails to perceive this phase.

(c) Full Operation: Your financial planning should consider the first twelve months of full scale operations, i.e., you're making sales and producing the product or service.

Let's assume Gearing-Up takes four months and you contemplate a Bridging period of two months. What I'm suggesting then is a financial plan that embraces the first eighteen months of your venture.

(2) Make certain your pro forma Profit & Loss and Cash-Flow computations are realistic and include all pertinent items. To this end, I suggest you arbitrarily overstate expenses and understate income by 10% each.

Ask your banker to let you review the latest Robert Morris studies. These compilations (by type and size of business) are presented in both balance sheet and profit & loss format and show the financial experience of other businesses in your field. It will be most helpful to measure your pro formas against this data. (Your banker uses these statistics in the analysis of a company's credit.) These studies also define and explain the various financial ratios. I urge you to utilize this publication in the consideration of your venture!

After you think you've "got it all down," ask your banker and/or CPA to go over your pro formas with you. (I recall an instance where a man was having trouble projecting acceptable earnings and was ready to abandon his project. His banker noticed he had included *debt service* [payments on principal] of $20,000 per year in the expense side of this P&L. That's a *cash flow* item and has no bearing on earnings per se.)

(3) Once you've completed your pro formas, the first thing you should do is increase your dollar (expenses) and time estimates by a quarter to half again as much! IT ALMOST ALWAYS COSTS MORE AND TAKES LONGER THAN YOU THINK! Getting lost? So am I! Let's do an example.

Assume your original projections indicate no income for the first four months of operation and costs of $25,000 or $6,250 per month.

$25,000 Original Cash Requirement
  2,500 Safety Margin of 10%
$27,500 Needed to Operate Four Months

I'm suggesting it could take *six* months and another $12,500!

$25,000 Original Cash Requirement
  2,500 Safety Margin of 10%
 12,500 Provision for Time and Dollar Overruns
$40,000 Minimum Financing to Begin

(4) The best time to *raise* money is when you *have* money! And that's at the *beginning* of the venture. It's so much more palatable to the investor (or lender), and easier for you, to talk in terms of *matching* your money. Money *already* invested by you in a venture is not as formidable as money you're *going* to invest.

(5) Try to go in with about fifty percent more than your most liberal estimate indicates you need. Staying with the num-

bers in the foregoing example, I'm suggesting a total figure of $60,000.

What we're talking about here is leverage, safety, and peace of mind. If you don't need it, you don't have to spend it. But at least you've got it (while the getting was good). These "surplus" funds might mean the difference between your investors losing what they've put up in a venture that collapses for lack of funds or being shareholders in a going concern.

This recommendation is not to imply that you shouldn't undertake your effort if you can't get together this kind of overage. I just want you to think about the rationale and plan accordingly. If you fail to raise enough, the results will be carried under that statistical column of businesses that fail because of undercapitalization.

(6) Exploit whatever leverage you can from the "trade." This can range anywhere from long term (90 day) payables to suppliers to actually trading some equity for goods and/or services. And don't neglect prospective clients or customers; especially if you're trying to get in a position of supplying them with a much needed product or service!

(7) Try to leave your personal credit unencumbered through the start-up. If things stumble, or completely fail, you'll need something upon which to fall back. Having credit capacity for personal needs will free your mind to concentrate on the venture.

(8) If possible, raise your start-up money via selling your friends, relatives, etc., stock vis-a-vis borrowing and signing notes. Better to give up some of the equity at this stage in exchange for no debts if the venture fails.

(9) Talk to knowledgeable people! Astute and successful business men would be my first choice. Investment bankers, commercial bankers, CPA's etc., all can be very helpful. You'll accomplish two very vital things via these discussions. Obviously, you'll get a lot of ideas and advice as well as perhaps having some hidden weak spots exposed. Secondly, by going to these people in the *beginning,* when you

have the venture before you and funds in the bank, you're going to get a lot more attention and help. When you've already exhausted your resources and are in difficulty, you're not nearly as welcome.

THE GOING CONCERN:

As indicated earlier, good, clean, reasonably priced going businesses are not easy to find. When they do become available, they're usually snapped up by friends (or relatives) of the owner(s) or by individuals or companies who are always in the market and are immediately capable of financially handling the purchase. Thus, the average person rarely gets a chance at the "cream." Nonetheless, one never knows, so it's time well spent to comment on this "method" of getting into business for yourself.

(1) Your first objective is, quite naturally, a thorough and exhaustive investigation of *all aspects* of the company.

Research in this area should impact first and hardest on the company's financial statements and federal income tax returns for the past five years. If the financial statements are unaudited, it would be an excellent idea to review them with the company's bank to ascertain if they reflect the bank's experience with the company. The best advice you can have in the area, however, is your CPA's.

(2) The next important step, and one very often overlooked, is to verify the largest customers. One way to do this , at the appropriate time, is to request that you and the owner of the company make joint calls on these customers.

(3) Thirdly, you will, of course, want to assure yourself of the operating condition of all equipment.

(4) Don't forget to verify the company's suppliers so you're assured of the availability of adequate "feed-stock" for the operation at proper price levels.

(5) The legal aspects of acquiring a going concern are most important! Don't be your own attorney (even if you are one) or use someone just because he's a good friend. Get a "pro." One thing you'll want to do is make certain you cut off all

liability to you as to previous acts, known and *unknown*, by the seller. You may want and need to form a new corporation for protection. Or perhaps an indemnity from the seller will suffice, if you're assured he'll have the wherewithal to make good on an indemnity.

(6) Just a word of caution regarding the verification recommendations above. Quite obviously these are very delicate areas and must be approached with the utmost tact and diplomacy. When do you make the approaches? The best answer I can give you, as a general statement, is to say, you'll know when.

If the seller is telling the truth about his operation, and you're polite, sincere and respectful in your conduct, he'll be happy to assist you in verification. If he has a problem with verification, you may have a bigger problem. Don't ever buy the old story about poor record keeping, slow accountants, and extended tax returns. What that often means is there *are* no records to verify. In such an instance, all you should be considering is perhaps an opportunity to buy some *assets* for a start-up operation; which raises the fundamental issue of whether it's better to buy stock or assets. However, since we're attempting to deal with the *going* concern here as a viable entity or vehicle, I feel it inappropriate to open up this "can of worms." I mention the subject only to identify a possibility for the acquisition of assets should various factors rule out purchase of stock.

(7) Financing the acquisition of a going concern is, generally, much easier than raising equity capital for a start-up situation. I'm sure that's obvious. You have stock (with assets behind that stock) to pledge, an earnings record, a proven product or service, customers, goodwill, etc. Owner-seller financing is one of the most attractive aspects of a going concern. The severe tax consequences of an outright sale for cash most often prompts an owner to sell on an installment basis. He personally carries notes for a portion of the purchase price which enables him to spread his tax bill over a period of years which means he pays less taxes.

(8) Beware of the so-called turn-around situation. These are often very tough propositions once you get into them. To be sure, there are many legitimate causes for a business not doing well; causes that are realistically (and sometimes easily) reversible. More often than not, however, companies in this category have irreversible problems that are not readily apparent or easily identifiable.

Should you decide the acquisition of a going concern is the most advantageous way for you to proceed, make use of all the professional talent available to you. There are reputable business brokers, investment bankers, and commercial bankers who can assist you in locating a business purchase opportunity. CPA's, attorneys, commercial bankers, etc., should be fully utilized in evaluating a candidate company.

SOURCES OF FUNDS:

(1) Friends and Relatives:

Unless you have money of your own, this is the only realistic source from which you'll be able to raise equity money for a start-up, as well as a portion, if not all, of your working capital.

Remember, it's always preferrable to ask people to *match* money you put in. The matching *ratio* (2 to 1, 5 to 1, 10 to 1, etc.) can/will be whatever your particular situation demands/commands. One way to approach the matter is to first divide the amount of money you're trying to raise by one-half the number of people you plan to approach (*all* the people you ask will not invest). Let the resulting figure represent the amount you contribute and, in turn, ask each potential investor to match. In any case, try to get at least two dollars for every one you put in. I like to try for a ten to one ratio; which means I have to plan to talk with twenty people and hope ten will go.

The best way to hedge against the probability of unfulfilled investor pledges as they relate to the timing of your plan is this. Say you want to be ready to get the venture underway in 90 days; set 60 days as a goal for having all funds *in the bank*. When a prospective investor agrees to participate, tell him you'll be back on a specific date with his stock certificate, etc., to pick up his check. I don't care *how* close the relationship is . . . never, never proceed on a promise.

Finally, there are some interesting tax benefits available to private investors in small business operations, e.g., a limited partnership, a subchapter S corporation and Section 12.44 of the IRS code. You should check these possibilities with your tax advisor.

(2) Commercial Banks:

They provide *working capital,* period! For the average small business operator, commercial bank lending generally involves "the temporary substitution of something he already has."

There are many ways in which banks can supply these funds, both as to the collateral required and the time or length of repayment. Short term lending usually involves loans for inventory and accounts receivable as well as unsecured loans to the extent your credit warrants such a loan. Medium to Long Term loans are made for such purposes as purchasing equipment, the financing of real estate and leasing of equipment. *Under certain circumstances,* unsecured term loans are possible for an entrepreneur to obtain. These circumstances include a bank (or banker) that *understands* and *practices* term lending and an entrepreneur who is well known to the banker, has an obviously viable deal and who can come up with about half of the venture's cost.

I encourage you to discuss specific ways and means relative to your venture with your local banker(s).

(3) The Small Business Administration (SBA):

The SBA is a federally funded agency that not only makes direct loans but also guarantees loans made by commercial banks. Apparently, its ability to make the direct loan depends on how much money it has at any given time from its appropriations. Recently, there seems to have been more activity on the loan guaranty side. The best procedure is to talk with your commercial banker. If his bank is interested in SBA loans, he'll be able to brief you on the procedures for applying. Generally, in loan guaranty situations, the commercial banker prefers to present your loan package to the SBA himself. However, I would recommend that you ask to accompany him for the simple reason that *you* know more about your deal than he does. A commercial bank is going to be more interested in an SBA situation when their loan demand is down and vice versa.

I'm not certain that *anyone* is qualified to tell you what the SBA will or won't do. I hear stories that range from large loans being made to financially substantial people to small loans being turned down for the "little fellow." But, don't let anyone kid you. The SBA is a collateral lender, pure and simple. If you don't have collateral, forget it.

In the event you decide to try the SBA route, you should know that there may be a federally funded private organization in your area whose purpose is to assist you in the preparation of a loan package for the SBA. They may also be a good source of information as to what the local SBA is currently approving, which loan officer is the best one to see, etc., etc. Call the local SBA and ask them if such a private operation exists in the local area.

(4) Small Business Investment Companies (SBIC's):

If you have a *fantastic* start-up situation or are acquiring a going concern that holds great promise, this is a possible source of both investment capital and loans.

If you have an unusually good venture, an SBIC will want to take stock in return for the needed capital. If your situation is marginal, they will probably prefer to go the loan route. The most likely arrangement is for an SBIC to make a loan in the form of a note (debenture) that is convertible into common stock at their option sometime in the future. The idea is obvious. If the company really does well, they'll convert and be stockholders in a successful company. If the venture experiences problems, they'll elect to remain as a creditor. The thing you want to be careful of is how much of the company you give up. This is where the pros (CPA, attorney, investment banker, commercial banker, etc.) can be helpful.

Most SBIC's are looking for a return on their money of somewhere in the range of three to six times the amount involved over a three to five year period. Their goal may be even higher in a start-up situation.

Functioning in somewhat the same manner are companies called Minority Enterprise Small Business Companies (MESBIC's). The purpose of the MESBIC, as the name implies, is to make equity investments in minority owned ventures. There are reportedly some eighty or so MESBIC's operating today. My understanding is that their policies may be more liberal than an SBIC. You can locate these companies through reference books in the public library, your commercial banker or the SBA.

(5) Commercial Finance Companies:

Essentially, these concerns make the same type of loan a commercial bank makes. The basic difference is their interest rates are higher since they're usually lending in higher risk situations than commercial banks are willing to consider. But, there's nothing wrong with that if you need the money.

Their method of lending also varies with the commercial bank, e.g., they buy account receivables outright rather than lending against them as collateral as does the commercial bank.

(6) Life Insurance Companies:

Possibilities for start-up are limited to borrowing against the cash value of a life insurance policy.

(7) CPA Firms:

While I don't wish to imply that all firms are "active" sources for investment dollars, I do know there are some who have recently been recommending investments in closely-held corporations of promise to tax burdened clients.

The best procedure here would be to talk with the tax partner in charge of the firm's local office.

(8) Factors:

Their function is lending working capital via an outright purchase from you of your accounts receivable. Usually, they will only advance you something like 60% to 80% of the receivable. The remainder is paid to you when the factor receives full payment. For their services, they charge a fee for each receivable plus an interest charge on the amount of money advanced to you. The fee and the interest rate may appear small, but when you compute the result in terms of annual rate of interest the figure is substantial!

Factors can be an excellent source of financing when you need them. However, you should discuss your accounts receivable situation with your commercial banker first. If he can't handle them for you, ask him to recommend a reputable factor. Also, he'll be glad to advise you regarding the terms offered by the factor and compute for you the true annual rate of interest you'll be paying.

In all fairness to the factor, I must add that he's entitled to a higher rate of interest than a bank on at least two very important points. First of all, the factor buys your paper without recourse to you. If there are losses, he takes them. Secondly, he has the job of billing and collecting. So, don't be misled by my statement of high interest rates or charges. Factors have a decided and very legitimate function in commerce. And you could well find yourself very, very glad to be in a relationship with a good factor.

(9) Money Brokers, Finders and Consultants:

The best advice I can offer you in this area is *know the person with whom you're dealing!!* There are many reputable people who make their living finding money for deals. And, in the search for money, you may well want to pursue this possibility. Generally, the finder commands a fee of 1% to 5% on a sliding scale relative to the amount found, e.g., 5% on the 1st X thousand, 4% on the next X thousand, etc.

Two things to watch for, however. Never pay any money "upfront," out of your pocket, for someone to find you money. Pay the finder's fee out of the money found for you. Secondly, make sure you know the source of the money ... make certain it's "clean" money. You don't want to wake up some morning and find you're sleeping with trouble.

———— o ————

What potential rate of return will attract the money you need? There are alternate forms of investment for the dollars you seek and the investor (or lender) decides where his money goes on a risk-reward scale; the higher the risk, the higher the potential reward must be. Approximate lending rates are quickly determined with a phone call to the prospective lender. What the equity investor wants to earn on his money is less easily ascertained. Generally speaking, however, he looks for an annual pre-tax return on his investment of from 30% to 60% compounded annually. The expected return varies proportionately with two factors; the growth stage of the company at the time of investment and the length of time the funds are invested. For instance, the start-up investment over a five-year period would command the highest return.

While you may not find that friends and relatives (know to) *expect* this high a return of their investment in your venture, it's good for you to know what equity money goes for in the market place. Secondly, you should want to offer them a higher profit potential than "public" investments such as savings accounts, C.D.'s, corporate or municipal bonds, listed stocks, etc., offer. (I should think twenty percent, pre-tax, would be a minimum today.)

LENDER RELATIONS:

You will be involved with the lending community, to one degree or another, throughout your business life. Understanding them and learning how to work with them is obviously most important if you are to generate maximum assistance, in whatever form, from this group.

Since the average reader will be dealing, the majority of the time, with commercial banks, this section is slanted in that direction. However, most of the topics discussed apply equally to any lender.

What your lender thinks about you will determine what he's willing to do for you. Character is the first, and one of the most important, things a lender considers. Loans that "shouldn't" be made, often are, simply because the lender "knows" his loan is good. Conversely, loan requests that offer 500% collateral are turned down because the lender knows he's going to have problems, of one kind or another, with the borrower.

(1) How Much Should You Borrow:

First, borrow *enough*. You've heard this said a thousand times. And it's true. If you're dealing, for example, with a *knowledgeable* commercial banker, he'll make certain you don't go in too short. He knows the last thing you need to be doing is spending good energy worrying about cash shortages. He, and you, want those energies directed productively into the affairs of your business. On the other hand, don't fall prey to accepting a loan of less than you *know* you need! What you set yourself up for, by borrowing too little, is just losing money that, somehow, you're going to have to pay back!

There's great temptation to let yourself be talked down to a borrowing level that does nothing but almost guarantee failure. In other words, the tendency is to take what you can get and try to run with it. Don't. If you can't get what you know you need, you're better off throwing in the towel than just going more deeply into debt.

The first concern of a lender is repayment. If you go in with a request for too little, he may make the judgement that you're not a good businessman and not lend you anything; thus, it's both financially and psychologically sound to ask for all you need if not a little more!!

You can, of course, borrow *too* much. What's too much? Too much is *any* amount that either (a) permits you to continue a losing proposition or (b) encourages you to expand an operation at an imprudent rate that, in turn, forces you into a position of insolvency.

(2) Educate Your Lender:

Be prepared to *educate* your financial "partners." The worst mistake you can make is to assume a lender (or investor) understands the economics of *your* (proposed) business. And a lot of people are not going to admit they don't know. Especially if you approach them on the basis that *you think* they know. That means they *should* know. Why should they "appear" to be stupid. It's much easier for them to say they aren't interested.

The natural tendency is for a financial person to stay with or repeat those situations he has successfully handled before. He's comfortable there. But, he had to learn those. So, he can learn yours. Make it easy for him ... and you! Obviously, the Business Plan or Loan Package can be of significant help.

Being thoroughly prepared, ready and willing to educate can serve another important purpose; separating the financial "clerks" from the sophisticated and creative "financier." If after a few minutes into your presentation, the presentees eyes sort of glaze, he begins interrupting you with unrelated comments about policy and answering his phone at every ring, you better pack it up right then. Even if you're successful in getting him to go along initially, he'll let you down at a later and more critical point. Not only because he doesn't understand; he doesn't *want* to understand. There are, unfortunately, far more clerks loose in pin stripes than the kind of financial person you've got to find. And they're to be found. You just have to look.

(3) Be Persistent:

If you've really got something good, don't give up on the financing after the first two or three tries. If you feel that you've been turned down by clerks, the remedy is obvious. Keep looking for a heavyweight. If you haven't already talked with some businessmen whose operations seem to be moving ahead, do so. Ask them who their financial "partners" are. In most instances, people are more than happy to make referrals. If, on the other hand, you feel you've talked with and been turned down by some knowledgeable financial people, ask yourself this question. "Do I know and understand WHY I was turned down?" Let's digress for just a moment.

When you present your deal, make sure you understand what's being said to you. Don't hesitate to interrupt and ask for clarification and definitions. If, upon being turned down, you still don't (quite) understand why, ask what changes or factors would *make* your deal a good one? Even if you think you understand what's "wrong," you still ought to pin it down by saying, "As I understand it then, you'd be willing to go along if A,B,C,D, etc ... am I correct?" With this approach, you'll learn how your deal should or could be structured and whether or not it's possible for you to handle.

I can't emphasize too strongly the *fact* that every financial person, regardless of his area of specialization in finance, is a little "different." Some people like this kind of deal, others don't. One man may have just "lost a ton" on your type of undertaking while the fellow across the street may love the situation you have. Some people welcome new ideas, others have severe chest pains at the thought. Even within the same institution, there are wide variances.

What I've said here is not to be construed as a recommendation to "shop" your deal all over town. Quite the contrary. But when you're just beginning, it's a little different situation than when you're at an advanced stage of financing.

(4) Get A Commitment:

Submit an application for a loan before you invest too much time and lay too many plans on the basis of what a lender *says* he will do. That isn't to imply, necessarily, that lenders make a practice of kidding you around. They don't ... maliciously or purposely. But, some people prefer to encourage you rather than close off a possibility until they see the situation in writing and have a chance to fully get into it. And they're absolutely justified in doing so. However, it's the *manner* in which they do it that can be a problem. They'll say something like, "Yes, I don't think we'd have any problem with something like that" and off you go thinking you have it made. If they don't add, "but, get all your data together and let me consider it," you "add it" for them. That way, you guard against any reticence he may have to step up and say no, or a difference of opinion and/or policy of his loan committee and any ineptness or error on your part to fully and accurately set forth your proposition. The saddest exchange of words between borrower and lender are, "but you said you would" and "but I didn't understand."

(5) Communicate & Perform:

Always ... do what you say you'll do. Or, if you see ahead of time you can't possibly perform, that's the time to go in and discuss it. Don't wait until the note is due to go in and explain that something which happened two months ago precludes your being able to meet the obligation today.

The cardinal sin is letting an obligation go past due and having the lender call you. Unless you're dead, or in the intensive care, there's no legitimate explanation or excuse. And it needn't happen.

Remember your financial partner's basic concern is getting *repaid*. If you've reached your wits end and can't handle an obligation, the *last thing* he's going to do is immediately try to force you into bankruptcy. He, for his own sake, is going to try and find all sorts of ways to help you pay him back.

(6) Rates and Deposits:

It may be "fashionable" to trade for the lowest rate of interest and keep your excess cash working for you in interest bearing time situations, such as treasury bills, commercial paper, CD's, etc. But, until you reach a stage where a point or two of interest on a loan rate or the dollars earned from "working" excess cash becomes significant, you're not being very smart, as a practical matter, to haggle over rates or keep your demand account down as low as possible.

Here's what I'm talking about. Say you're borrowing $30,000 and the rate is 8½%, but you only need the funds for six months, so your interest expense is $1,275. O.K., you hear from a friend that he borrows money for 7½% "all day long." The next thing your banker knows, he's being accused of ripping you off for one point. I mean, 1% is 1%! But, what *is* 1% in terms of dollars in this example? It's a staggering $150! Over the six months, it's $25 per month! Less than $1.00 a day!

And how about that $5,000 average balance in the company's checking account. It's just lying there. Let's put it to work, that's the smart thing to do. O.K., you put it in something that yields, say 6% per annum. That's only $300 (pre-tax) a year. Less than $1.00 a day!

I hope what I'm trying to say is obvious. You need a good relationship with your lender. Don't let the "big boys" make you paranoid about idle cash and points. Otherwise, you'll find yourself "running over dollars to pick up dimes."

(7) Compensating Balances:

Commercial banks are in business to make money. (It's coincidental that they make a portion of their money via loans). In order to grow, they must have an ever increasing inventory (money) to "rent." Where does this inventory growth come from? A continuing flow of new depositors. But, these new depositors also will have loan needs. If all a bank does is lend its full limit, it has no funds left to attract new loan customers. Growth stops. This is an oversimplified explanation of why banks often require what's known as a compensating balance. For example (in additon to all the other requirements attendant to making a loan), the bank may require the borrower to agree to keep, on demand deposit, cash equal to 20% of the amount borrowed.

It is customery, certainly legal, and most understandable if you relate the foregoing explanation. My point is, don't take up the hue and cry of the uninformed who run around screaming, "hell, if I had those dollars, I wouldn't need to be borrowing them, etc., etc. That's going to get you absolutely zero. Either understand it and accept it or, shop your loan around and maybe you can find a banker who won't require compensating balances. (When loan demand is light, banks are more lenient and vice-versa.) The banker is a human being who, just like you, wants to be understood and appreciated. You're asking him to understand *your* needs and lend you money for your company to grow. At least (pretend to) reciprocate that understanding. If you do, you'll be a fresh breeze across his desk and he'll bend over backwards to help you.

BANKRUPTCY:

This is never a pleasant subject to contemplate ... until you need it. Then it's "nice to have around." And that's the purpose of this section ... just to let you know relief is available and to suggest what *your* approach should be to it.

In the event it ever becomes impossible for you to satisfy the demands of your creditors, it isn't necessary to subject yourself, and whatever value remains in the company, to abuse or harrassment. Under Chapter 11 of the Federal Bankruptcy Act, a company can be permitted to operate, protected from creditor lawsuits, while working out a plan to pay it's debts.

The procedure for dealing formally with creditors is really quite simple. You lay the matter squarely in the hands of your attorney (and that includes any proposal by you or a creditor to enter into any kind of written agreement/settlement).

VI

MARKETING/SALES

Have a death wish? Just ignore, or even take lightly, this area and you'll succeed in spades! There is no faster or more certain route to failure than a lack of capability in or understanding of these vital functions.

This would appear evident without having to mention it. Then why do I? Because a significant number of failures can be easily traced to poor performance in marketing and sales. Obviously *something* is amiss when something so obvious so often becomes the Achilles' heel of the entreprenuer. Here's the scenario I believe occurs and is responsible for this phenomenon of overlooking the obvious.

Let's go back to the proposition that all entrepreneurial efforts are rooted in fantasy. Okay. There you are: the entrepreneur . . . flushed with dreams of wealth and fame and independence . . . in short . . . success!! I mean, *you* sure as hell think your idea is great or you wouldn't be pursuing it, right? A substantial part of the reason you think your undertaking is super is because you've *already* determined, at least *in your mind,* that others will, or do already, want what you've got! And this is where "it" happens! Right here! At this critical point, it's remarkably easy to say to yourself, "Of course, marketing and sales are important. But, that's just a matter of routine. I've got to first get the financing solved, the corporation formed, set up my offices, etc."

Well, my friend, . . . it's not a sleeping dog you're letting lie . . . it's a Bengal tiger. He's a light sleeper and be assured he'll awaken. You can't know how difficult it is to function with 600 pounds of cat on your back. (The breath is unreal if nothing else.) THIS is the time to GET OFF YOUR BUTT . . . get your head out of those proverbial clouds and *make damn sure:*

(a) **Who** wants it.

(b) **Where** they are.

(c) **How** you can reach them.

(d) **Who else** is offering **what else.**

There's an old, and true, story about the man who developed a new dog food. His organization, financing, production, marketing, packaging, advertising, sales were all first rate. Only one problem . . . the dogs wouldn't eat his product! Very simple, very basic, you say. Right. But it happened!

Early on, then, develop a new and healthy respect for marketing/sales. If you don't know, or can't remember the basic or traditional channels of distribution, learn them quickly. Particularly the *economics* attendant thereto. A close friend had everything set to market his product through retail department stores. That is, he had called a couple of buyers and talked with some "knowledgeable" friends. He found that retailers usually mark up 40% off *retail*. His arithmetic indicated his cost would permit a price to retailers which, when the 40% was applied, would produce a competitive retail price. Great. He had it made! Wrong! After his entire operation was based on this distribution channel, he discovered: (a) he had to co-op the cost of advertising with the retailer (b) sales were *consignment* sales (c) he had no control, or voice, in the display position of his product (d) he had to service and maintain his product on a weekly basis (e) he had to lay in a minimum inventory of $3000 (at his cost) and (f) he would receive payment for what the store sold on something like a 45-day period following the sales. He didn't have the capital to begin, let alone sustain, such an operation with the twenty-five stores he planned all along would be his base . . . his bread and butter. Another dream shattered.

MARKET RESEARCH:

There are four methods of researching markets. (a) The Public Library (b) Professional Marketing Firms or Consultants (c) The Trade (or prospective customers, themselves) (d) The "Competition."

(1) The Public Library:

This is the first place I go. Unless you've spent any time recently in your public library, you'll be amazed at the range of services many can provide. At the very least, you'll be amazed at the information it's possible to obtain . . . *If You Know How to Use a Library!!* If you haven't spent much time in one, believe me . . . you *don't* know how. Librarians, for the most part, are extraordinarily dedicated people. Dedicated to serving the public. They want to help. They can help. Just walk in and introduce yourself to the head librarian. Tell him or her why you're there and that you need assistance in using their facilities. You want to learn how to use a library properly. And then look out! Dedication + training + recognition of an oft overlooked and underrated profession = a ton of assistance and data!

While I'm certainly no "pro" at using the library, here's a small example of what *not* to do. Let's say you're interested in the restaurant business. So, you walk in and look in the basic card catalog for books on Restaurants. Say there are 20 books listed. (Let's be ridiculous and pretend all 20 are on the shelf at the same time.) O.K. You scan read them and pick up whatever looks interesting. Can you believe how many people stop right there? They assume they've seen all the available books on the subject. How many people know there are reference books entitled "Books in Print." By subject matter, by author, and by title! Every library has them. Sit down and go thru one. You'll be surprised at the number of references and cross references to your subject.

71

Another excellent reason for beginning with the library is that you need to accumulate sufficient background data on your subject to intelligently discuss it with other people.

Lastly, it often can save you from running head long down a rabbit trail. I've been dissuaded from proceeding further on a couple of ideas because the evidence I found in the library was overwhelming against any chance for success.

A note of caution regarding "authoritative" data. Make certain any data upon which you base important decisions is *objective*. Once, the key determining factor for a go-ahead in one of our operations was based upon statistical data gathered from the official annual publication of the industry. We discovered too late that the publisher was also in the business of selling mailing lists and his statistics were almost 100% too high. Instead of a hard core market of 10,000, there turned out to be only 5,000!! We fell prey to the clever use of semantics and categorizing techniques. Actually, we had only ourselves to blame. We could have dug just a little deeper and found the truth. But that damn volume was so "official" and we had stars in our eyes. (Which quickly turned to holes in our pockets.)

(2) Professional Marketing Consultants:

The first step is, of course, to determine competence. If you don't know a first rate consultant, you can call on two or three; tell them what you have in mind and ask them to write a proposal for you. (The proposal should always be accompanied by references, including current and/or former clients.) Or, if you have the connections, don't hesitate to ask friends in large companies who they have used. Thirdly, and particularly if you don't live in a large city, you might inquire through the professional marketing associations in the field in which you're interested. Another excellent source is the marketing department of a college or university. They can be very helpful.

A word of caution about consultants. There are many excellent professional marketing firms and consultants in this country. There are also the "Xerox" operators. The latter operate by supplying you basic data available to anyone and it's very general in nature. Then there are those who seem to have no original thoughts and simply parrot back to you what you said to them. This may be an ego trip for you, but that's about all it'll be.

You can get a pretty good feel about his capability from just talking with a consultant. In your discussion, I would not waste either his time or yours by telling him all *your* plans or thoughts. You're there for him to help you. Let his proposal represent his original and objective thoughts. Secondly, I want to run anytime I hear a professional (in any field) say to me, ''what is it that you'd like for me to do for you.'' I want them to tell me what I should have! That's how it ought to work. I tell the accounting firm I need a cost accounting system and they ask me what I want it to be capable of doing? Indeed! How absurd can you be. *Tell* me what it should do . . . what I ought to have!

Finally, I would suggest you do the other recommended research yourself before you consider using the pros. Some time and effort on your part should produce at least the essence of a feasibility study. If *your* work indicates a feasibility, then you may wish to go forward with a professional to determine breadth of market and specificity of approach.

The competent and recognized professional practicioner can also be of immense help where one is faced with making a strong case in the financial area. Lenders and investors can be greatly influenced by a first rate marketing study which indicates a strong possibility for success!

(3) The Trade or Prospective Customers:

Testing. That's what we're talking about here. And that's the essence, in the final analysis, of success or failure. Why bright and otherwise competent people discount testing is hard to understand. But, again, it goes right back to that fantasy stage. They just are so convinced they know what somebody wants or will buy.

I thought I had sufficient information about a product I wanted to market to the schools of this country. I knew they used the product. I knew they had bought the proposed product in the past. I prepared a pro-forma based on 75,000 public schools, 20% of which I could sell, in an 18 month period, an average sale of $50.00. That's 15,000 sales $50.00 or $750,000. I also talked with a couple of friends who were professional educators and they thought I had a super idea. Their only criticism was that I should figure on $100 average sale. Wow, $1,500,000!

I based a couple of major decisions on this market and made a go-determination which entailed a projected 120 days of work at a cost of $5,000. Four months later, I realized I was in deep trouble. I was correct on my estimate of 20%. (In fact, it turned out to be about a 30% positive response. Positive in the sense that 30% said they would be interested.) The problem was two-fold however. Almost 100% would not be able to purchase for anywhere from 6 to 12 months and the average sale was about $10.00! In other words, the market was just not there to command a significant part of our overall capability or plans for profits. The sad thing was, my secretary could have told me had I asked her. I mean if I had asked her to spend a few days and a few hundred dollars in long distance calls to talk with a hundred or so schools around the country. Of course, the above experience involved a low cost item with volume as the key. Phone calls and/or a test mailing would have produced the necessary results, and saved me $5,000 and four months of work.

In those instances where you have a relatively expensive product or service coupled with a somewhat limited market, you should consider a totally different approach. Let's say the product is a computer soft-ware package for banks. Call on several banks. Is your package really needed? Does it do the job? Will the price be acceptable/competitive? How fast or slow are they to move? Does it take a top management decision? Are there other allegiances of the bank that will prevent them from doing business with you? etc., etc.

To make the important point another way, your *prospective customer can tell you, without any doubt, whether you'll succeed or fail.* If you'll ask him. Incidentally, I would suggest you prepare a questionnaire for (your) use in such a survey. In addition to reminding yourself of all the pertinent questions you should ask, a questionnaire can serve an even greater purpose. It's an invaluable ''self interrogation'' tool. Careful preparation of a comprehensive questionnaire can be remarkably helpful in revealing hidden flaws to you in your overall plans for the project.

(4) Competition:

It has many faces. It can, in some instances, ''make'' you; in others it can destroy you. In any event, it is an area which should be of intense concern to you. We all hear the "big boys" say, "I love competition." I kinda think that statement, taken in the purest sense, is ridiculous. Indeed! Can any of us honestly say we wouldn't like to "corner the market" on something? I would. You would too. So, let's deal with reality.

Reality number one is that if you really and truly have no competition the day you start, you better know you're *going* to. The minute the market place gets wind of anything that simply *appears* to be profitable, "they" are going to be in there with both feet! Thus, where you have something new, your plans should consider these two elements. First, keep as low a profile as long as possible. Resist the urge to tell people what a *gold mine* you have. The "trade" or industry . . . is always quick to spread the story of a "goer." The longer you can make them think you're just getting by the better off you'll be. For example, an acquaintance really found the "mother lode" after about 10 months of operation. He immediately layed on a celebrative and thank-you dinner for his trade credit people announcing to one and all that now he could go on a 2/10 net 30 basis. (He had been 60, sometimes 90 days. No interest or other charges had been made for that leverage. His trade credit was happy.) Within two months, he had three strong competitors, all subsidiaries of large companies. They cut their prices almost below his cost. Within three months, one of them bought him out for a nuisance value price. Plan for competition to come. How will you deal with it? Can you deal with it effectively and quickly. Just be prepared for this inevitable occurrence.

The apparent *absence* of competition when you first look for it should make you extremely wary. *Why* is there no competition? There could be one of three reasons why you see none:

(a) You haven't *fully* investigated. (Don't, whatever you do, *ever* take anyone's word.)

(b) Others have tried and failed.

(c) You actually have a novel/unique product or service.

One good thing existing competition tells you is that your idea is viable! In fact, there's an old business axiom that says, the smart way is the tried way. In other words, why spend time, effort and money on something unproven. The risk is high; the chances of success low. Capitalize on the other man's risk, research, and product. Simply make it better and/or sell it for less and/or market it better.

As a practical matter, if we use the word competition loosely, it can be said that your "competitors" can and will openly assist you (toward success I mean). There are any number of situations where your trade area does not overlap with that of someone else in the same business. Even within the same city this can be true. Locale and type of customer are most often the "permissable" difference. For example, if you're considering the dry cleaning business, you should be able to talk with the "competition" about basic economics, problem areas, suppliers, etc. If you have to, you can go to another city or town and obtain first hand data. Trade associations can often be of great help as well.

If you're venturing in some purely creative field such as writing, sculpture, the crafts, etc., you'll usually find your peers are eager to help you.

Just a note of caution regarding the use of competition in market research. You can depend on hearing all the bitches about how tough it is to make it ... I don't care what your field is. People love to be martyrs. So don't be overly discouraged. *Something's* good about what they're doing or they'd be doing something else. Secondly, you can afford to be vague and you should be vague. Take the approach, "I don't know the first thing about what I'm doing. I'm just trying to find out." This way you don't give away any "secrets" and you certainly don't represent a threat (as a novice). Just listen. It's excellent market research data.

Regardless of what kind of product(s) or service(s) you'll be offering, it has its own best (and worst) selling periods. And, there are good and bad months for selling anything. Again, you say, "he's telling us what we already know." O.K. It's simple and it's basic. But it's also frequently ignored in the white heat of discovery and getting going.

ADVERTISING:

Obviously, no specificity is possible without a precise product or service as a point of reference. However, there is an important point to be made in this area and we can make it by defining the word advertising to mean "telling people you have something to sell." Using this definition, it's virtually impossible for anyone to say they don't have at least some need for advertising. The important point, therefore, is how *are* people going to find out you have something to sell? It's a consideration that you best not leave just to chance.

The level, the specific type(s), the cost, the frequency, the methods are all relative to your specific product or service and the industry in which you operate. Using my admittedly primitive definition, look around at your competitors. How are *they* telling people they have something to sell? This can be an excellent point of departure from which to begin formulating whatever advertising plan(s) you need.

Of course, the best basic advertising is to turn out a superior product or service. This is what produces the coveted "word of mouth" advertising. But, depending upon the business you're in, this may well not be sufficient in relation to your specific goals.

Each type of undertaking has its own set of advertising secrets or criteria or rules of thumb. For example, does the *location* of your type of business make any difference? If it does, that means being in the right place is a form of telling people you have something to sell. Thus, *location* can be spelled, a-d-v-e-r-t-i-s-i-n-g!

Advertising is often a whipping boy, sometimes misunderstood, frequently done poorly, defiant of quantification in terms of results, and a hundred other negatives people find to lay at its door. But, you have to tell people you've got something to sell ... and that's the strongest case I can make for advertising.

In concluding this section, I'd like to explode a common myth, about the average small business not being able to avail itself of some of the talent that exists in the better agencies. The "excuse" is, the advertising budget isn't big enough to interest those agencies. Well, that's true ... they're not going to be interested in handling, per se, a small account. But, consider this possibility. Arrange an appointment to see the manager or director of one of these agencies. Tell him straight out you only have X dollars in your proposed budget and realize his agency isn't interested in you as a client. However, what you'd like to do is spend part of your budget to buy two or three hours of his time for the purpose of having him give you some basic advice and direction. (And that basic direction should include a recommendation of a new or small firm of capable people who would be more than pleased to have your account.) The dollars you spend on this opportunity to pick the brain of a first class advertising talent could be a bargain.

THE "NEW" MARKETING:

As a final thought in this marketing section, I'd like to share something with you that I've found to be most intriguing and very profitable. Whether or not your product or service would lend itself to this marketing method is for you to decide. If it does, fine. If not, I think you'll find the proposition interesting anyway.

One of the most misunderstood methods of moving goods and services is Direct Mail/Mail Order. (Direct Mail refers to mailing a solicitation to buy directly to a prospective buyer while Mail Order solicits via advertisements in newspapers, magazines, etc.) There's a tendency for the uninformed to "look down" on this method of selling. Ironically, Direct Mail/Mail Order (DM/MO) is the most sophisticated form of marketing we have today and is used, to a greater or lesser degree, by virtually *every* consumer oriented industry in the country! Why? Because it's extremely efficient and highly profitable! From the major oil companies to the finest jewelry name in the U.S. . . . . the smallest local restaurant to the largest bank ... they all are involved in DM/MO in one way or another. For example, you may not view receiving a catalog from a posh department store as that firm's involvement in selling by direct mail ... but that's exactly what it is. Or, how about a bank's program of bank-by-mail. Think they're not using DM/MO as a marketing tool? Of course, they are.

The reason DM/MO is often overlooked in marketing plans is simply because the planners don't really understand the economics or the principles involved. The simple, but often elusive, basic proposition is the extraordinarily high return on investment realizable in *successive* years from repeat sales to customers obtained in prior years. This occurs because of the very *low cost* to mail to *customers* plus a high % response from customers relative to the *high cost* of mailing *to prospects* and the low % response from mailing to prospects. By comparing the two following columns one can more easily see how this occurs.

ANNUAL RESULTS[1]

	Mailing to Prospects	Mailing to Customers
No. Mailed to	240,000	9,600
% Response	2%	15%
No. of Sales (responses)	4,800	1,440
Price per Sale	$ 20	$ 20
Gross Income	$ 96,000	$28,800
Less: Cost of Goods	19,500	5,760
Gross Profit	$ 76,500	$23,040
Less: Cost of Mail	43,200*	1,800*
Balance	$ 33,300	$21,240
Less: Overhead (25%)	24,000	7,200
Net Profit	$ 9,300	$14,040
Return on Investment	10%	95%

*Here's the big difference ... $43,200 in mailing costs to get $96,000 Gross

vs.

$1,800 in mailing costs to get $28,800 Gross

[1] These figures represent an actual case. However, the reader should be aware that the product was a *repeat* product i.e., people would buy one or more, several times a year. You are also cautioned that the percentage response figures only represent the results in this specific case and should not be construed as a benchmark.

-NOW-

The progression, in Net Profits, over five years works this way:

Each year, the 240,000 are mailed to new prospects and *each* year, you get back 4,800 responses or customers to whom you mail *twice* each successive year ... and it just "snowballs." For example ... in round numbers:

	2nd Year	3rd Year	4th Year	5th Year
No. Customers Mailed to (Twice)	9,600	19,000	28,600	37,200
Net Profit Contrib.	$14,000	$29,000	$45,000	$58,000

Well, I hope you found the foregoing food for thought. I should emphasize, however, that it would be the most serious of mistakes for you to view the results of the project I've just shared as anything but an effort to simply whet your appetite and arouse your curiosity. If you think your product or service might profitably lend itself to DM/MO, you have a tremendous amount of research ahead of you before you're ready to even seriously consider the implementation of such a marketing vehicle.

Should you wish to pursue the possibility of DM/MO, I suggest you do two things. First, get in touch with the Direct Mail/Marketing Association, Inc., 6 East 43rd Street, New York, N.Y. 10017, and ask them to recommend some basic reading material. Secondly, secure a copy or two of the monthly trade magazine "Direct Marketing" which will begin to give you an idea of the scope and sophistication of the industry. Finally, if you really get interested, there are periodic seminars you can attend, DM/MO consultants to advise you and advertising agencies that specialize in DM/MO.

SALES:

It may seem patronizing to begin this section by saying your product or service is worth nothing if you can't sell it. O.K., but there are a tremendous number of people who (after the fact, sadly enough) would say their failure might well have been averted had they been a little more basic in their approach to a sales program.

Obviously, I cannot provide a specific prescription for a well-rounded sales effort in a book not directed to any given product or service. What I can do is offer some random thoughts that will hopefully provoke your attention to and consideration of how you *will* come to grips with the specifics of the sales effort you will have to make.

At this stage, let's assume your marketing research efforts have determined demand, primary and secondary markets, competition, and a basic marketing approach. So, now it's a matter of deciding *how* this marketing plan will be implemented, which, in turn, dictates *who*, what kind of person, will be required to execute the plan. And here is where the seeds of a troublesome, if not failing, sales effort are often sown. A mis-match of the *how* and the *who*.

First, let's deal with a sales program that requires person-to-person selling and assume *you* are neither experienced in sales nor wish to perform the role of principal salesman on a day-to-day basis. Your first decision then is going to involve whether you think a successful sales effort can only be conducted by an in-house salesman or is sales success possible via a non-staff representative. In either instance, will your product and service, coupled with earnings potential, present a promising enough package to attract the caliber salesman necessary to affect sales at the required pace to achieve success. Let's say you determine a need for in-house capability and can answer in the affirmative to the questions in the preceding sentence. There's still one key question to be answered . . . what *caliber* salesman do you need? If you aren't really certain . . . if you're not experienced in sales . . . I urge you to seek assistance from a reputable sales consultant. Discuss your product or service, your basic marketing thrust and ask for a recommendation as to what kind of person should be employed, what kind of deal you should make and where such people are most likely to be found. I'm not suggesting you should or must take the consultants advice. Rather, I'm submitting a recommendation for an independent sounding board. You must come up with an effective combination of the right person to sell to the selected market.

Well, up to this point, we've been assuming your proposed venture can afford a sales capability other than just you. Yet, there are certainly a predominate number of ventures where the entrepreneur himself *is* the sales force and that's where he makes it. He's a great salesman. But, what of an instance such as we talked about in Chapter IV where selling is abhorrent to you? What are your alternatives in that case? You have two realistic options. Either you'll be able to reconfigure your deal to afford the required sales capability or you abandon your venture. That may sound negative or too harsh but we're talking about making a venture successful; not a scheme to lose money. The latter is what you will have been a participant in if you make the wrong decision about sales.

Records are extremely important in the sales function. They not only have important financial, tax and accounting implications, but form the basis upon which marketing decisions are made, how sales people perform and are paid, what production considerations are necessary, etc. In fact, your sales records are your primary navigational aid in the venture. In this sense, they should be able to tell you where you've been, whether or not you're on schedule and serve as your flight plan for where you're attempting to go.

It is often said about sales (and marketing), "you're only limited by your imagination." I think that's true. So many times, the difference between poor, good and outstanding success is found in the entrepreneur's ability to conceive and execute marketing and sales programs.

To be sure, sales and marketing are relatively inexact sciences, and innovation, coupled with good people, usually increase the results of a given effort. However, there are proven fundamental sales techniques that anyone can learn and effectively apply regardless of the product or service involved. There may be more good books, manuals, and courses available on sales than any other aspect of business. I urge you to avail yourself of these aids at the earliest possible point in your venture. *Persistent* and intelligent utilization of good basic salesmanship will produce sales!

PRICING:

This area was one of the greatest single frustrations in my first venture. Pricing is something that requires constant examination and attention. How much is enough ... how much is too little ... how long should a price remain ... can you justify to the buyer a higher price than your competitor ... could you sell more for less and see an increase on the bottom line (or vice versa) ... if you charge less to A than you do to B, will you have inordinate problems with B, etc., etc.

I view pricing as both a science and an art ... depending on who does it, with what product or service, in what industry, with what results financially. Pricing situations range from "what the market will bear" (in the case of a new item) to a very narrow margin for price differential in a highly competitive market with a standard product or service. The former is most complex with the latter being almost clerical in nature.

There are any number of "rules of thumb" used in pricing e.g., if you're manufacturing and retailing, your retail price should be a minimum of four times your manufacturing cost. However, you should never apply rules of thumb blindly. Four things will guide you toward your price: (a) Competition (b) Costs (c) Pricing practices within your specific industry (d) What the market will pay. The one immutable law of pricing is to absolutely know *all* your costs!

Since I can't tell you specifically what to charge, the only purpose of this brief section is to "red-flag" a vital aspect of any venture that somehow seems to get less attention than it deserves in the initial going. If I've created concern, and subsequent action, my purpose has been accomplished.

VII

PRODUCTION

The eternal battle. Production people complain that sales and management promise too much too soon. Sales and management scream that they're losing sales to competitors and spending their time dealing with irate customers, etc. Well, it's not that bad, usually. But there will always be some degree of disenchantment, one with the other. Because basic goals as well as personalities and temperaments are different. The solution is to minimize these differences. And you minimize most effectively by going in with good equipment, known capacity and good people. Those three, coupled with good procedures, communications and understanding will operate to your maximum benefit.

Since the higher percentage of entrepreneurs fall into the category of management, sales, and marketing orientation ("picking up" the production function either via a "partner" or sub-contractor) we'll deal with production from that point of view. And, while much of what we'll say about production is "cast" in the light of a product, most of it is quite appropriate to a service.

If you make a major mistake about production in your organizational stage of the enterprise, it's going to surface late and deadly. It will fall upon you just about the time sales really begin to build and nothing is so disheartening after all you've been through to that point. It can keep you a bridesmaid forever. Here are some things to think about that will be helpful in precluding such a possibility.

(1) In-House Production:

Let's assume you and a production man are putting a venture together. Up to this point, about all you've done is have a great deal of conversation regarding what he knows about the product and what he says can be done. He's as enthusiastic about the venture as you are. But the real impetus behind the deal is you. *Now* is the appropriate time to "prove up" the production aspects that you've been discussing. *Before* the company is formed, financing arranged, deals set, etc.

(a) Make inquiries in the industry about your production man. Ascertain his experience (with what kind of equipment) work habits, schedule completion, etc.

(b) In a situation where the equipment already belongs to the production man, make certain that it is technically capable of producing the product and is in excellent working condition.

(c) Thoroughly familiarize yourself with the various types of equipment that will be used or are available (on the market) for use. How subject is it to down-time, obsolescence, simplicity of operation, etc. What do your prospective competitors use and why. How much of the sales pitch involves the type of equipment used, etc.

(d) Realistic production capability should be reflected in your pro formas. For example, you should not estimate that 100% of your equipment will be in production 100% of the time. It won't.

(e) Back-up or alternative production capability should be part of your overall planning. How will you handle unexpected down-time and/or occasional jobs too large for your equipment.

(f) Cost of Goods Sold. *You* must take the responsibility for making certain that *every* cost is recognized and properly priced.

Don't just ask your production man how much it's going to cost and accept a lump-sum figure. What you want to see is a break-out of all the components of that figure. You should probably provide him with a sample costing schedule. (These may be available from your CPA or perhaps the appropriate trade association will be able to provide you with some helpful data.) Also, you should consider discussing the subject with one of your competitors or someone in a closely allied field.

(g) Feed Stock. Make certain of your sources of raw material. Not only in terms of how plentiful it is, but how available it will continue to be. How about timing and delivery? Is there any appreciable risk that your supplier(s) could so control the market for what you need that they could virtually dictate prices to you?

The basic message regarding in-house production is this. Production people are *production* oriented. They are not necessarily good businessmen or managers in the sense of taking an overall operation forward. Nor should they be expected to perform in that manner. It's *your* job to provide the production man with the wherewithal he needs based upon your astute evaluation and understanding of those needs in relationship to *all other factors of the operation*. I'll undoubtedly alienate some fine people in production when I liken their role in a venture to that of the chief engineer aboard a ship. True, without propulsion the ship goes nowhere. But, it's the captain of the vessel who is responsible for the voyage, makes it possible and must ultimately call the shots. That's you.

(2) Sub-Contracting Production:

The comments in this section are equally appropriate for the In-House operation. Even if it appears, initially, that you'll never have any need for an outside capability, you should think alternatively. What if you *do*? Is it even available? If so, where and at what cost, and what time problems would there be, etc., etc. Have a back-up!

Obviously, the first thing you're going to have to do is educate yourself to the extent of being able to converse intelligently about the production of your product. At this stage, you should consider obtaining the services of a consultant who could advise you with regard to securing a sub-contractor(s). In addition to basic and initial consulting, you might even want him to *participate* with you in the negotiation of any contracts, etc. You might also plan to utilize his services after the operation is up and going whenever you're faced with a situation in which you felt uncomfortable or inadequate.

The following aspects of handling production on a sub-contract or farm-out basis should be carefully considered if you're to have a smooth and profitable operation.

(a) Of course, you'll want to get bids. What's new about that? Nothing. Except make certain in the comparison of these bids that you're comparing apples with apples. And price alone shouldn't, of course, be the final determinant. The *best all-around deal* is what you're looking for. And that may have little tc do with price. I'd rather pay more and know I could depend on a schedule than less and be running around like a crazed camel wondering if I could deliver what I'd sold!

(b) Quality is also an obvious consideration. Most people can produce an acceptable prototype or "first batch" of goods. But can they *sustain* your minimum requirements. Make certain you nail down (a) *quality* of raw material (b) desired production procedure and technique and (c) performance specifications of the completed product or service.

(c) Test runs by your prospective supplier, if the situation lends itself thereto, can be extremely important. In other words, see if they can perform as they say they can.

(d) On-sight visits to proposed production facilities are an absolute must. Assure yourself that they have the equipment they claim and that it's operational. And people! Do they have the qualified personnel necessary? You can tell a great deal about the operation (you're considering as an integral part of your venture) by just spending a day or two in the offices and plant.

(e) Contracts. Whether or not your arrangement necessitates a formal contract depends on many factors. In any event, I suggest you at least approach the question *thinking* contract and let the attendent facts (together with your attorney) determine that one *isn't* necessary. Common sense says the greater degree of reliance you must place on a sole or given sub-contractor for the success of your venture, the more likely you are to want a contractual arrangement. If you can switch subs easily with no disturbance of your overall operation, the less important a contract might be.

(f) The financial strength and/or status of a production capability will be important to you. If they're weak in this area, it reduces the amount of leverage you may need and want in the form of trade credit and/or financial participation in other forms. Secondly, you run the risk with a financially shaky supplier that he will experience difficulties that can manifest themselves in higher prices to you because he has high credit costs. And, of course, he could go under and create massive problems for you.

Your commercial banker will probably be glad to assist you in checking the credit of prospective sub-contractors, and don't be reticent about asking for references in the form of other clients or customers.

(g) Trade credit will, or should, form an important part of your overall financial picture. What you want to try and effect is a situation where you don't have to pay until you've been paid, and still benefit from discounts allowed for early payment! One way to approach this, if you have a sufficiently sophisticated sub, is through a letter of credit. I told a contractor it would take me 90 days to convert my receivables into cash and I wanted the same 90 days in which to pay him. I also wanted the 2% discount he offered if his invoices were paid in 10 days! I offered then to secure my position with a letter of credit from my bank with which he could, in turn, use to borrow against if his receivables from my new and untried company could not be discounted at his bank. He wanted my business and, under those fully secured circumstances, agreed to let me have the 2% discount. I had a certificate of deposit at 5% interest that I pledged to my bank to secure the letter of credit. The cost of the letter was 1½%. (Thus, I had "earnings" for 90 days of 7% less 1½% or a net of 5½%.)

(h) Communications with your supplier are vital. If you find it expedient to place orders by phone, be absolutely fanatical about following up with a detailed written order. Anytime telephone conversations involve costs, prices, material changes, time and delivery factors, etc., always follow up with a letter, e.g., "In accordance with our phone conversation today, I understand A, B, C, D, etc., etc. If I've misunderstood or misquoted any aspect of our conversation, please let me know immediately." Whenever service to you falls short of the agreed basis, come right on down on those folks. I don't mean in a rude or nasty manner; just be certain they know you're on top of the situation and that you care.

If you'll establish and faithfully maintain good communications along these suggested lines, you'll minimize problems. When your supplier has to make a choice (when he's in a jam) as to which of his customers he's going to give preference, you want it to be you. What you don't want to be is "good guy" Sam. Sam always gets the "oh, that's Sam, he'll never squawk" routine. And that kind of reputation will filter through your supplier's entire organization. The production line, packing, traffic, shipping, credit, administration, etc., etc. You can be rightfully "demanding" without being repulsive. You can be a "good guy" without getting walked all over, too. Set the stage properly going in and it'll pay big dividends.

VIII

MANAGEMENT CONSIDERATIONS

If you're experienced in management you will, of course, be familiar with most of what's contained in this chapter. However, it may serve a couple of purposes for you. First, in the sense that it will reaffirm the necessity for certain administrative practices as they relate to an entrepreneurial undertaking. In addition, there may be one or two new ideas you'll find helpful.

For the person without any, or very much, actual management experience, I hope you will be persuaded of the critical nature of the management function to success and seek whatever additional assistance you feel is necessary *before* you jump off.

TIME MANAGEMENT:

Time will be one of your greatest foes. Three things about time as it relates to venturing are irrefutable.

    (a) It screams by at an alarming rate relative to costs in general and payroll specifically.

(b) It seems never to pass in terms of getting things done and generating income.

(c) It always takes longer than you think.

The most critical area is the management of one's *own* time. You've got to plan it, organize it, and execute. And the real key to success here is constant re-organizing and re-planning! In addition to providing yourself with a time-framed and sequenced plan from which to operate, you'll find good and consistent planning of even greater value. A well-conceived and maintained Plan of Action will provide you with a sense of power to the extent that you'll feel in command of things. You will have an excellent over-view of "how-goes-it," you'll be far less hassled, and your anxiety level will be greatly reduced.

PLANS OF ACTION:

The success or failure of a Plan of Action will serve as a beautiful indicator of where changes need to be made. Plans of Action usually fail for one or two reasons. First, because they may not have been realistic as to timing and response from *others*. Secondly, you may have overrated your own abilities or capacities. In the latter instance, you'll have an invaluable analytical tool to assist you in determining *how* to take *what* remedial action. For example, let's say mailings were always delayed and sales calls were falling behind. Obviously, you have to hire someone if the level of activity you're attempting to maintain is considered to be minimum. Where are *your* talents most productive? Make that judgment and hire the opposite talent. (In this example, you might also discover how undercapitalized you are. Or, such a situation could be indicative of your distaste for sales.)

So that we don't become lost in semantics, let's take a moment to specifically and graphically define what I'm referring to as a Plan of Action.

THE PLAN OF ACTION:

Is a three-part plan:

(1) **Long Term**—Annual/Quarterly

(2) **Intermediate**—Monthly

(3) **Short Term**—Daily/Weekly

Each component above is detailed to a lessor or greater degree with:

(1) **What** will happen

(2) **When** it will happen

(3) **How** it will happen

And each of these goals/targets is then over-laid in terms of:

(1) **Time**

(2) **Income**

(3) **Expense**

Obviously, it's broad and general to begin with; increasing in specificity as the time "frame" under consideration lessens; what might be called an inverted pyramid approach.

Look as if we're getting into a massive quantifying project? We're not. To be certain, you're going to have to put in some time to think a good Plan of Action through and commit it to paper. But you *must* plan, whatever you call it. What I'm suggesting here is a method to organize your plan and a road map to execute it. Here's how I do it.

By the time I'm ready to prepare a Plan of Action, I already have my financial and marketing pro formas. I know where I'd at least *like* to be 12 months down the road in terms of completed projects, sales, earnings, cash flow, etc.

(1) Annual/Quarterly:

Break the year into quarters with particular attention to markets; the high and low periods. I usually find major project completion lends itself to quarterly planning. Revise this portion of the plan (at least) quarterly. (Be certain you stay within the orginal 12 months at each revision unless you move your original 12 month pro formas out to a longer time period.)

(2) Monthly:

The monthly segments major function is to give you a tracking base for what you wish to accomplish quarterly. In other words I try and break down to a monthly level, for the 1st quarter only deadlines for various steps that must occur. This is where I really start to zero in; tying myself to target dates ... seeing if they make sense ... if they're realistic. I revise this part of the plan either monthly or when events occur that make revision obvious.

(3) Daily/Weekly

The Daily/Weekly Plan is the "truth and the light." This is what you'll work from on a daily basis. This is where you'll fail or succeed in your management of time. And your management of time may well determine *ultimate* success or failure!

This is the "work" I take home at night. I've found spending a half hour or so every other evening regrouping does several very important things for me. I *do* really know where I am at any given time; which means I know what I have to do and what the priorities should be. Secondly, I very often solve problems via this re-grouping process. Most importantly, I think, it produces a very positive attitude. I mean, whether times are rough or smooth at least I know what's happening. Thus the limiting effect of anxiety, which often comes from fear of the unknown, is lessened appreciably. I'm "free" to concentrate all my energy on solving rather than guessing and fearing. (I've always told my wife I would be happy to do something about that noise outside in the dark if I really *knew* what was out there. Most times, I just crawl down under the covers and try to forget. Other times, I've been shamed into nearly blowing my foot off or beating a fallen pine cone senseless. Finally got smart and installed outside flood lights. At least, I can *see* what the hell is going on.)

There are two other tools I find most helpful in the management of time and self. A 2' x 3' calendar that displays an entire year by months and days. I can *see* the whole 12 months in which I'm operating. To this calendar, I log project deadlines from the Plan of Action. The second is a plain old black board. Mine is 3' x 6'. This is where I work out problems of various kinds. Work flow, financial strategies, etc.

RECORDS:

Poor record keeping can seriously impair a venture for any number of reasons ... financial, marketing, sales, costs, legal, accounting ... you name it. Unless you've run an operation before you aren't going to know at the outset everything you will need and want to do in this area. Some will be immediately obvious; others won't. Some you start to maintain will be found useless; others you may see no need for until months after you've begun operating.

For many, the biggest single fault is failure to *maintain* records. It's an easy trap in which to fall. But poor maintenance is only symptomatic of a far more serious problem ... your inattention to or lack of knowledge about what's going on! You can't read and analyze something that doesn't exist!

The simplest answer to proper maintenance and timely use (by you) of records is to assign up-keep to clerical people. AND, set a specific time each week that you will review management information produced by your records. In the heat of battle, records are the easiest thing to procrastinate about. But, if your clerical person(s) knows you're expecting up-dates, say each Monday morning at 9:00 a.m., they'll be there.

Your best source of what kinds of records are needed in the basic areas of finance, taxation and legal matters is your CPA/accountant/bookkeeper. And there are many excellent books and other publications which speak directly to recordation for small businesses. Records that produce marketing and sales management information are, to some degree at least, a matter of common sense. And it is the principal area where trial and error may be the best teacher. It has usually been my experience that I set up system X to gather data ABCD from which management report Y is derived only to discover at a later date:

(1) The information is interesting, but I can't react timely.

(2) The report is incomplete because I neglected to include this, that, or the other.

(3) I don't need this or that part of the report anymore.

(4) I only need these figures monthly instead of daily, etc.

The key point I wish to make about records and the management information produced from them is this. Success depends upon your ability to make right decisions. The more accurately informed you are, the better your decisions will be. And you're going to be as well informed as your records are current and complete.

Lastly, a word of advice and caution regarding records, data and decision making. You will never have *complete* data. To try and quantify *everything* before making a decision is impossible and efforts to do so will be detrimental. You must have, or develop, the ability to know when you've seen enough, make your decision and move on it.

PERSONNEL:

It's pretty well established that people hire in their own images. This could be good or it could be very bad. The answer is, of course, hire what you know you need. Similar life styles, philosophies, education, etc., are not, within themselves, reasons for employing anyone. On the other hand, you don't need the trauma that comes from *sharply* mis-matched personalities. Somewhere in the middle is where you want to be.

Make certain each member of your staff has a written job description as well as the oft-neglected job standards. It's fine to tell the typist one of her duties is to type letters. But, you should also tell her what *level* of performance you're paying her for. What's acceptable? One, two, three errors ... no errors?

I always try to pay a person just a little more than they can earn elsewhere at the same job. And I emphasize what I'm doing. If the operation reaches a point where a profit sharing arrangment can be set up, I do so. But I'm wary of talking big, or at all, until I'm ready to deliver in this area. Otherwise, I'll create an atmosphere of "failure," or trouble at the very least, when I can't follow through.

In preparing financial pro formas, I always include some sort of Christmas bonus for people. But again, I don't tell them ahead of time. (Remember, I'm already paying them more than they can make elsewhere.)

Where do you find good people? Every employer bitches and moans about this. I think that's sometimes just talk or, in many instances, simply a lack of good thinking. There are several extraordinarily good places to look for people who are trained, trainable, capable, anxious to work and highly productive.

(1) The Senior Citizen:

Without a doubt, this is the greatest waste of a natural resource this country has. This is a group of people, who, if just given the opportunity, will out class a whole bunch of us younger and "more qualified" folks. You ... I ... we, make the senior citizen "undesirable" by our silly rules and policies.

There's a great "hidden" advantage to taking on the person over 60 or 65 ... you can *learn* from them, if you're willing. They've been there and back, so to say, and it's a shame for all that experience and know-how to go unused. And do they *want* to use it! If you're interested, and I hope you are, call a local senior citizens group.

(2) The Armed Forces Retiree:

Great talent! Some of these people are just in their early to mid-forties and many of them have had management and supervisory experience most of us civilian executives have never had (and may never have). A call to the local recruiting office is probably the best way to locate prospects. Tell the ranking NCO what you're about then he'll be able to recommend a procedure to locate people. If that fails, try advertising in the service newspapers, e.g. The Navy Times, etc. Your public library can tell you how to get in touch with these publications.

(3) The 40+ "Failure":

These are people over 40 who I refer to as "failures" *only* because they, for whatever reason, are no longer ensconced in a corporate rocket ship to the top. There are hundreds of perfectly legitimate reasons why they're available. To overlook this group is to ignore some of the finest talent available in this country. If you're interested, and don't personally know anyone in this category, try calling a Plus 40 Club in your area.

(4) The Divorced Woman:

Specifically, the woman who is say 35 to 45 years old . . . probably has children, a degree in some non-technical field and has spent the last 15 to 20 years running a household, doing civic work, etc. etc. At this point in her life, what she needs is a career and all she usually has offered to her are low paying, unskilled and dead-end jobs because she doesn't have any "experience." What she does have is maturity, a good mind, a tremendous desire to excel and loyalty to and for whomever steps up and offers her a chance.

(5) The Physically Handicapped:

Take a look, for instance, at any Goodwill operation and tell me handicapped people can't make a tremendous contribution to an organization.

(6) The Former Convict:

Obviously, I'm not talking about the hardened criminal. But, what about the thousands of people released every month from our penal institutions who have paid the price of some (dumb) mistake.

There are lots of good people wasting away on the outside (or headed back inside) because their record haunts them incessantly as they make the rounds of job opportunities. Your local law enforcement people can be of assistance if you're interested, or you can go directly to the state and/or federal level involved.

 o

There are several things all of the foregoing groups have in common that should be of keen interest to the entrepreneur.

(a) They're looking for a chance . . . an opportunity . . . and whoever provides it is going to get a super enthusiastic and loyal employee.

(b) They really *want* to work. This is the biggest problem I've found with a good many otherwise acceptable people.

(c) Relatively speaking, they aren't as career critical. That is, they aren't facing the interruption of a career with the high-risk opportunity you have to offer. They can afford to take a chance with you.

(d) For the most part, there's a wealth of experience in these groups. Maybe, in some cases, not precise experience, but motivation can make up a great deal of ground awfully quick.

In any event, I'd recommend you give yourself an opportunity to pick up some potential winners from one or more of these groups. You might find it a refreshing and profitable experience.

THE VOLUNTEER EXECUTIVE COMMITTEE:

I don't recall ever seeing a committee so entitled in any text or treatise on business. But, the rationale behind such a committee is this. I've always been more successful, doing whatever I did, when I had people around me who were smarter than I. People who at least could challenge, take issue, be the devil's advocate, infuse objectivity, remove the forest so the trees were visible, etc. Since most ventures start out small with capital not necessarily coming from knowledgeable and astute business people, the typical board of directors (if you have one) may be worthless to you in terms of assistance.

As an alternative, you might *consider* doing what I've done on occasion. But you must proceed carefully lest you create more problems for yourself than you solve (see "Friends," Chapter IV). Create an informal "executive committee" of three or so successful (business) people whom you know. Tell them you'd like to have their thinking and advice; ask them if they'd meet with you once a month over lunch to let you tell them how it's going and for them to point out to you anything they think you're overlooking. *If* you get the right people (or just *one* right person) they:

(1) Most likely will see (some of) those little hidden areas you miss because you're too close. Just a suggestion here or there can be extremely helpful.

(2) May become very enthusiastic and be a "ready made" potential investor group if things (1) do go well or (2) begin to falter, but the basic deal is still sound.

(3) May be very helpful in (timely) identifying when it's time to get out.

(4) Could be in an excellent position to assist you in getting back on your feet, in the event of failure.

Obviously then, such a "committee" could be of considerable value to you. But I stress again, *only* if you get the *right* people and are capable of properly handling such a situation.

I think you will be able to ascertain whether a volunteer executive committee is a realistic or desirable possibility for you. If you don't feel it's a particularly good idea, you'll be better served to leave it alone.

PROFESSIONAL RELATIONSHIPS:

I'll probably step on some toes here. But I don't really mind. I find the tenderest toes belong to the least informed and least competent. And that's what I'd like to have you avoid in the selection of those who represent you in legal, tax, accounting and other matters requiring professional attention.

It is false economy, and poor thinking (of the first order) to have someone represent you simply because he's a friend, has a license, won't charge as much, etc. Search out the "pro." Pay him what he charges. You'll never be sorry.

The specialist is often cheaper than the "generalist," on two counts. First, most everyone works on an hourly rate and the person who *knows* what he's doing can do it in less time. Secondly, the odds are you won't end up having to spend dollars later on to correct poor work or to financially bear the brunt thereof.

Think too about how substantial the professionals are whom you select. In other words, if they make a mistake, can they make restitution? I am *not* suggesting or even hinting at malpractice. If you're careful in your selection, my experience is that you probably don't have to worry about that. But, all of us make *mistakes*. And if you're damaged by a mistake, you ought to be made whole.

You'll find competent professionals who are pros at their specialties in large, medium and small firms. The only thought I have with respect to size is that there is always a psychological plus when you use a respected name. At least, a name that is worthy of respect even if it isn't a "household" word. Perhaps as your operation becomes increasingly successful, you may decide instant recognition is worth the change or at least the addition.

Remember, when dealing with attorneys, it's *advice* you're paying for, not decision making. You should never abrogate that vital function and, if you have a smart attorney, he isn't going to let you do it. Expect to hear the statement occasionally, "what you're asking me is a business judgment matter, not a legal question." At least, I hope you do, because that means your attorney is attempting to stay within the purvue of his function.

Some attorneys seem to be overly zealous in finding all the reasons why you can't or shouldn't. Others can spend massive amounts of time and your money trying to "out do" opposing counsel in the putting together of a deal; sometimes to the point of actually killing it.

No, I'm not anti-lawyer. What I *am* saying is, attorneys, just like all of us, have different approaches to the accomplishment of their jobs. What every client needs to ascertain, sooner or later, is what modus operandi works best for him in a legal relationship and seek out the attorney who "practices that kind of law."

ORGANIZATION:

Organizational form is, of course, the province of your legal counsel. You should be guided by their recommendations. However, here are some thoughts to keep in mind.

The *simpler* your organizational structure, the better. Much to do is made of the protection against liability a corporate form of business provides. Maybe, in some cases, too much. Discuss it with your attorney. He may tell you that in a "one man" operation, the corporate shell isn't that effective. For example, if your new corporation borrows money, the bank will insist that you sign the note *personally* as well as president of the corporation. This is a good example of the rationale that holds that a person can not avoid liability in the altogether sense just by the creation of a legal entity. So, at least have some dialogue with your attorney about the pro's and con's of a corporation.

Partnerships per se, bear the closest scrutiny of all. There are thousands of successful operations carried on in this manner. Particularly where the partnership consists of several partners. But there must be thousands of unsuccessful partnerships where only two equal partners are involved. Maybe it's O.K. for you and whomever; all I'm suggesting is, you both ought to really think about what you're doing. Don't just "get it on" because you "get along." Because you just might not always . . . get along.

In an instance where two people, for whatever personal or other reason, just have to be 50-50, so to say, your attorney should be consulted regarding alternatives to a partnership or a 50-50 corporation. For example, each of you might form a corporation and have your respective companies enter into agreements with the other to effectively carry out the intent of your venture. I know, this runs counter to the simplicity of organization I espoused earlier. But, almost anything is better, to my mind, than a standoff situation between two equally empowered individuals who have come to despise each other. The wish for infant mortality will, I assure you, appear most pleasant by comparison.

Should you determine the formation of a corporation is the best route, ask your attorney and your CPA about the advisability of what's called sub-chapter S corporation or election. Very simply, you can elect, under sub-chapter S of the Internal Revenue Code, to be taxed as an individual vis-a-vis as a corporation. While there can be problems with a sub-chapter S corporation, there are also some excellent tax benefits to be derived. The basic rationale of sub-chapter S is that since most small businesses lose money initially, it is preferable to be able to use any losses against income in your personal tax return.

If you're putting money into the venture, you should also ask your CPA or tax attorney whether it's better to (a) lend the money to the company and take a note, (b) inject the funds via the purchase of stock or (c) pay for expenses out of your pocket and bill the company.

COMMUNICATIONS:

Good communications may not make your venture successful, but poor communications can cause serious damage. Most of the problems human beings experience (whether they're business, marital, financial, political, etc.) are a result of poor communications.

The faster your operation grows, the bigger your communication problem(s) will become; rapid growth always demands more and better, but is a natural deterrent to it. Over and over again, management consultants, called in to solve problems, ultimately identify poor communications as a prime culprit.

Regardless of what type or size operation you have, there are four aspects of good *internal* communications that should be incorporated from the outset.

(1) Job descriptions and *standards* should be written for each job.

(2) A procedure manual should be developed which articulates (and flow-charts, if applicable) the various functions involved in the operation. For example, the shipping department should have a detailed, step by step, routine to follow beginning with the moment an item to be shipped enters that department (or stage) until it's dropped in the mail or handed to a carrier. Likewise, what happens from the moment an order is received until it hits the production department, etc., should be routinized.

I like to think of procedure in terms of a long, straight conveyor belt. As the total function of processing an order moves down this straight line, each stage (of completion) generates the need for peripheral action, e.g., recordation, reorder, notification, financing, purchasing, etc. Developing formal procedures forces you to visualize your operation and thus provides an excellent opportunity for you to properly *relate* all the aspects thereof.

Another important use of a well-designed procedure is in the area of trouble-shooting. If you have an indicator to follow or trace when something goes wrong, the problem is more easily and quickly found.

But it isn't enough to simply *say* this, that and the other will occur in this order, at this time, etc. What many procedure manuals ignore is the *human element*. Just because you *say* thus and so will occur doesn't mean it *will*. Because good ole Charlie may just not do it. So, be sure you build into your system checks that recognize this fact and "override" non-performance. For example, a procedure for use of company vehicles may require the driver to notify the motor pool before he leaves with the vehicle. But, somehow, they

103

never do. Instead, people just take the keys off the board and go. Alright, change the procedure to require that all keys will be kept in the manager's office so drivers are *forced* to observe the notification rule. That's a very simple example to be sure . . . but it illustrates the point.

(3) Staff meetings once a week are essential to good communications as well as morale. Even if there are just two of you in the operation, it's good to sit down over a cup, review the past week and look ahead to the next. If there are several people to be included, it's always a good practice to try and have an agenda of some sort to follow.

Sometimes, however, staff meetings can be counterproductive. For example, the person in charge is dictatorial, over-bearing and permits no participation from others. Or, staff members are constantly held up to ridicule before their peers. If your staff meetings begin to seem useless and strained, the solution may not lie in discontinuing the meeting. Let it first be a signal to you, the conductor of the meeting, to take a good hard look at yourself! Could be you have bigger problems developing than just a meeting that doesn't "come off."

(4) Write it down . . . or most of it. Whether it's a question or a directive . . . if it's important . . . black and white is an excellent color combination for a smooth running operation. I'm not talking about long, exhaustive, detailed, dictated memoranda. Lay in a supply of half-sheet size, three part, snap-out memo forms that have a place for your message at the top and space for a reply at the bottom. And, *handwrite* them! I've found I can say what I want to say in about a tenth of the time by jotting it down in longhand.

As far as *external* communications go, just a couple of words. First, remember whoever answers your phones *is* your company. I'll never understand why some people seem to almost insist on carrying the totally unnecessary liability of rude, cold, uninformed greetings to callers. Don't you have enough problems anyway? And think seriously about not having your calls screened. I mean you're either there or you're not, and how many nuisance calls do you get everyday and how long do they take? In other words, who do you think you are? Recently, the president of a Fortune 500 company (who takes all his calls) said, "when I get to be God, maybe I'll need some help. Till then, any person who cares enough to take his time to call me, I've got time to talk to him."

An interesting statistic would be the amount of business lost every year because the caller just got fed up with, "may I ask who's calling and the nature of your call." The caller just hangs up and the *callee* never even knows he has just lost a multi-thousand dollar piece of business! The other side of the "phone-coin" is your out-going calls. The man who has his secretary place his local calls with the announcement "Mr. Jones? Please hold the line for Mr. Smith," has got to have a business death wish operating. How absurd can you be? I don't care who you are (or think you are) there's no excuse for this. If I respond at all to such calls, other than by simply hanging up, it's just to tell the secretary to have Mr. Smith call me back when he has time to talk (and then I hang up).

Incoming correspondence should be responded to within a maximum of three days after receipt. If an actual response, for whatever reason, is impossible, then a brief note acknowledging receipt and promising a response should be sent. It takes less than five minutes for a steno to get off such a note and it's really just a matter of simple courtesy. But, in this day of impersonality, such a practice will make an excellent impression.

Finally, there are communications experts available to you ranging from the no-cost telephone company pros to paid consultants whose area of expertise is the art of written business communications. All you have to do is recognize and acknowledge the importance of good communications and you'll be able to quickly decide what, if any, assistance you need.

INSURANCE:

The scope of insurance coverage will depend upon several things which include:

(a) The types of exposure to insurable risks your operation involves.

(b) Whatever insurance coverage might be legally required.

(c) The amount of risk *you* are willing to assume.

Whatever your financial situation may be or your basic attitude about insurance or your knowledge regarding the subject, you should *at least* counsel with a first rate insurance man.

While a relatively small number of people fail because they weren't properly insured, it doesn't help much if you're one of them!

IX

CONCLUSION

Being an entrepreneur isn't an easy road; nor is it, by any means, a certain one to financial rewards. You'll give up a great deal to go down this road; you may find it far too disagreeable and abandon it. But, it can be a grand super-highway with rewards undreamed of and unattainable in any other career mode.

Entrepreneurship offers a perpetual frontier to and for those who would risk the uncertain ... the unknown. It is, indeed, one of the precious few frontiers left in this world; one that discovery does not ... cannot ... diminish.

According to (some) city dwellers, there's a process through which one must go as a prerequisite to survival in the city ... it's called "getting street-wise." So it is in the business world ... especially the world of the entrepreneur. You have to get street-wise to make it. And while the coming of wisdom obliges experience, the severity of learning can be attenuated through guidance. Perhaps then to refer to this book as a "street guide" would not be inappropriate.

———— o ————

To summarize the opening point in this book, learn to stop and ask yourself this simple, short series of questions whenever you're faced with a critical problem in your venture.

(1) **Why** is it happening

(2) **What** should be done

(3) **Why** isn't it being done

(4) **Why** am *I* not doing it

(5) **What** would happen if I *did* it

———— o ————

Let me conclude with a brief personal story in an effort to impact the significance of these five key questions.

Some years ago, I organized a group for the purpose of acquiring a company in the eight figure range. We worked extremely hard for several months and had everything ready to go to the closing table within the week. The situation could not have been in better shape. The sellers were happy, our investor group was happy, the lawyers were happy, and I was exuberant. In a word, everything was perfect!

And then, without warning, it happened. The next day the country was plunged into the energy crisis. Ninety percent of our financial backing was oil money and that's where our funds went . . . to buy oil. There were massive and quick profits to be made and I couldn't really blame anyone. But there we were with an extraordinary opportunity and virtually no money.

Those of us who remained had one last chance to bring it off. We had to find sufficient non-oil money within two weeks or lose our chance to a listed company who was also interested and had the financing to go forward.

Six or seven days of frantic searching produced one legitimate possibility. An individual in the mid-west who was interested in the industry and hopefully "our" company. I finally established telephone contact with him five days from our deadline. No, he had not received the copy of our Business Plan I had mailed to him. Yes, he would talk with me for a few minutes because I came highly recommended by a mutual friend.

He listened attentively, asked some knowledgeable and probing questions and waited patiently as I desperately tried to answer, explain and persuade, all at the same time. I realized I had failed quite miserably when his last question clearly indicated he was viewing the basic premise of the acquisition in precisely the opposite light. "No sir," I said, "It's just the other way around."

"Oh, I see ... what you're saying is, the valve division, because of the depreciation aspect, represents the remainder of ..."

"Well ... in a way that's true. But, if we come back to simple bottom line figures, we uh ... well, you see you can't be ..."

"Oh, yeah," he agreeingly interrupted, "that's where it all comes home to rest ... the bottom line. Well, look. It really sounds as if you people have a very interesting deal, but I think I'll pass this time. I've got so many other irons in the fire ... maybe we can get together on something in the future ..."

We were dead and we knew it. We couldn't raise the money and that's *what* happened to a most promising venture.

Now ... let me tell you WHY we weren't successful. "We" blew it, obviously, because I chose to use the telephone rather than get myself up there to sit down with that man with all the facts and figures spread out before us. How absurd. Even my children understand they have a better chance of getting something if they "corner me" face to face!

Well, that's all fine and good but *WHY* didn't I go to see the prospective investor? Now we're beginning to get at the *real* reason I failed.

    (a) I was physically and mentally tired.

    (b) I was about, I thought, to come down with a "bug" of some kind.

    (c) Storm fronts were pushing across the country and I dislike flying in bad weather.

    (d) I was emotionally despondent.

    (e) I convinced myself that I should feel the man out by phone before making a two day trip.

I gave up ... that's what I did. Down deep I was feeling we weren't going to make it. I ceased to persevere and in so doing all of my excuses and reasons became the important issues and enfolded me in a comfortable blanket of justifiable failure. And I didn't get on an airplane.

The energy crisis (which by the way our old group still enjoys blaming) really had nothing to do with the failure. The real "crisis" was me!

Had I known to take myself through the simple analytical steps outlined above, I think I would have pulled it together and bought a plane ticket. If I had met personally with that man, I could have persuaded him to join us.

This "business" failure was, upon analysis, completely unnecessary. Since that fiasco, I've been able to surmount problems or potential problems of far greater magnitude by submitting the difficulty to the objective scrutiny of those five simple questions. That's precisely correct ... instead of indulging in the fatal practice of excuse mechanisms, I've learned to look within myself. Because that's what being an entrepreneur is all about ... YOU!

EPILOGUE

Three weeks to the day following my phone conversation to the prospective investor, he called to enthusiastically say he had just finished going over the Business Plan and hoped the situation was still a possibility. I had been only a plane ticket away.

BUSINESS PLAN
&
PRO FORMA CASH FLOW

BUSINESS PLAN

I. SUMMARY

    A. Description of Business
      1. Name
      2. Location and plant description
      3. Product
      4. Market and competition
      5. Management expertise
    B. Goals
    C. Earnings pro forma and estimated return to investors
    D. Summary of financial needs and application of funds

II. PRODUCTS OR SERVICES

    A. Description of product or service including patents,
       copyrights and legal and technical considerations
    B. Competitors' products

III. MARKET RESEARCH

    A. Description of total market
    B. Industry trends
    C. Competition
    D. Specific major and minor market(s)

IV. MANUFACTURING

    A. Materials
    B. Sources of Supply
    C. Production methods

V. MARKETING

    A. Basic strategy
    B. Pricing rationale & terms
    C. Channels of distribution
    D. Advertising

VI. MANAGEMENT DATA

    A. Form of business organization
    B. Board of Directors
    C. Officers: organization chart and responsibilities
    D. Resumes of key personnel & plans for staffing
    E. Facilities plan
    F. Plan of Action

VII. FINANCIAL DATA

    A. Financial history (five years)
    B. Five-year financial pro forma (quarterly for 1st year)
      1. Balance Sheet
      2. Profit and loss statements
      3. Cash flow projection
      4. Capital expenditure pro forma
    C. Explanation of pro formas
    D. Business ratios
    E. Explanation of use and effect of new funds
    F. Pro Forma R.O.I. (and relate to industry.)

XYZ COMPANY
PRO FORMA CASH FLOW

	1976		1977									
	Nov.	Dec.	Jan.	Feb.	Mar.	Apr.	May	June	July	Aug.	Sept.	Oct.
Investment	25,000											
Less: Start-up Costs	15,000											
Beginning cash	10,000	9,000	5,000	2,000	1,000	3,000	4,000	2,000	1,000	1,000	2,000	4,000
Sales (cash)	1,000	20,000	25,000	27,000	30,000	29,000	28,000	28,000	28,000	29,000	30,000	30,000
Acct. Rec. Collections	-0-	3,000	3,000	3,000	3,000	3,000	3,000	3,000	3,000	3,000	3,000	3,000
Loan Proceeds	10,000											
TOTAL Available Cash	21,000	32,000	33,000	32,000	34,000	35,000	35,000	33,000	32,000	33,000	35,000	37,000
Cash Disbursements												
Payments on Inventory	5,000	20,000	22,000	22,000	22,000	22,000	22,500	22,000	22,000	22,000	22,000	22,000
Owners Draw (A)	2,000	2,000	2,000	2,000	2,000	2,000	3,000	3,000	2,000	2,000	2,000	2,000
All Other G&A Exp. (B)	4,000	4,000	6,000	6,000	6,000	6,000	6,000	6,000	6,000	6,000	6,000	6,000
Purchase of Bus.	-0-											
Debt Service (C)	500	500	500	500	500	500	500	500	500	500	500	500
Depr. & Bad Debts	500	500	500	500	500	500	500	500	500	500	500	500
TOTAL Disbursements	12,000	27,000	31,000	31,000	31,000	31,000	33,000	32,000	31,000	31,000	31,000	31,000
Ending Cash (Cash Flow)	9,000	5,000	2,000	1,000	3,000	4,000	2,000	1,000	1,000	2,000	4,000	6,000
Cumulative Cash Flow		14,000	16,000	17,000	20,000	24,000	26,000	27,000	28,000	30,000	34,000	40,000

Notes:
(A) From the expense side of Profit & Loss Statement.
(B) If not a start-up.
(C) Principal (only) payments on Loan.